Anthea k

2009

There's a Bat in my Bedroom

Anthea Hanscomb

Published by

MELROSE BOOKS

An Imprint of Melrose Press Limited
St Thomas Place, Ely
Cambridgeshire
CB7 4GG, UK
www.melrosebooks.com

FIRST EDITION

Copyright © Anthea Hanscomb 2009

The Author asserts her moral right to
be identified as the author of this work

Cover designed by Catherine McIntyre

ISBN 978-1-906561-46-8

Printed and bound in United Kingdom by:
The MPG Books Group

This book is dedicated to the Pritchards of Tuffs Farm, Chipperfield,
Herts.

Without the help of Frank and Jim, we would never have done
as well as we did on our smallholding.

They came to the rescue when things went wrong and were
a fund of very useful advice.

Acknowledgements

My thanks to the late Mr John Boughton, who was a wealth of information about traction engines and the work that T T Boughtons of Little Chalfont did during the Second World War.

Thanks also to the late Jim Pritchard, who successfully jogged my failing memory; the eleventh edition of the *Encyclopaedia Britannica*; and Mr L D Craker for his input about thatching.

Jim Pritchard with Teddy, 1940.
He was a true countryman and gentleman.
Photo by Georgie Pritchard.

Introduction

When in 1931 we moved from London to Chipperfield in Hertfordshire, little did I dream that eight years later we would be at war with Germany. We had evacuees from North London and turned our five acres into a smallholding. My mother went in for rabbit breeding with twelve does and two bucks. With that number of does, there was a steady flow of young rabbits to the butcher. With the smallholding set up with hens and rabbits to begin with, followed by a cow and six sheep, I went to work at Tuffs Farm. It was an experience not to be missed! Frank Pritchard did all the work with the horses, about which I knew nothing! There were tractors on some of the bigger farms but even they had horses for the lighter jobs. There was a lot to learn and some of it was hard work, but there was never a dull moment, except for potato picking in the pouring rain and sprout picking when they were covered in snow! The only horse-drawn jobs I did not do were ploughing, mowing and reaper/binder. In those days everything was grown organically, the only chemicals were sulphate of ammonia as a top dressing and nitro chalk for acid soils. No pesticides or herbicides and we grew excellent crops! I had twenty years of wonderful country life which I have missed ever since!

Anthea Hanscomb
25 August 2008

Chapter One

"Don't, whatever happens, let Kiwi out," announced my mother. Kiwi was our cat and he was sitting on a chair in the kitchen, busily licking off the butter my mother had smeared down his back and on his paws. "That is to keep him occupied while all this upheaval goes on," she explained.

It was August 1931 and we had just moved from London to Chipperfield in Hertfordshire – two town-bred children and a six-year-old town-bred cat. I knew nothing of the countryside. I was born in Birkenhead in 1920 and a year later my parents moved to London, where my brother John was born in 1926. Kensington Gardens and Hyde Park were our nearest bits of greenery and as a special treat we would go to Richmond Park in the summer. At least we were familiar with horses because in London we had seen them every day pulling the coal carts, the rubbish carts, the Express Dairy milk float and many delivery vans.

Though I was fascinated by the milk float horse, which always knew where to go and when to stop, my favourite pastime was watching a beautiful Aveling and Porter steamroller whenever the roads round South Kensington were being repaired. I was a steam enthusiast from a very early age.

Chipperfield proved to be very different from London. We were delighted to be free in a large garden of our own. It had thick hedges in which we could hide, several lawns, trees we could climb, fruit trees galore and a massive tangle of blackberry bushes. It was a totally different way of life: no traffic noises, and a deafening dawn chorus which took me weeks to get used to. Also gas lighting, which I didn't dare touch for at least a year. There were one or two surprises in store and at the end of the first few months I did wonder if I would get used to living in the country.

First it was the flea. Whippendell House had been owned by a woman who bred dogs. They had been given the run of the house and there were fleas in plenty. Fortunately they were discovered by the decorators before we moved in and fumigation cleared all but one. It plagued us for about two weeks, choosing a different bed each night. Finally, I caught it in my bed and drowned it in the bathroom basin.

Then there was an enormous spider, which was found in the spare bedroom. I was terrified. I had never seen anything so big, except at the Zoo. My mother finally caught it and put it outside. Next day it was back in the spare room, where it remained for the three years we were in that house. Every evening it would come out of the room and thump its way along the corridor. It didn't walk quickly, and if we were feeling brave we would try to turn it round, using a newspaper; and send it back to its home behind the gas fire. My father, who had been terrified by a camel spider in Mesopotamia, would have killed it but for my mother, who always quoted, "If you want to live and thrive, let a spider run alive." So we accepted the spider and became used to its antics, but some of our visitors were not too happy when they found it in the bedroom!

The next surprise was being stung by a queen wasp, which had managed to crawl into my bed. She, no doubt, thought she had found the best possible place in which to hibernate. Wasps had been seen in London of course, but not in any great numbers and I had never been stung. The queen was killed: a huge fat wasp which squelched on the floor when trodden on by my father; and a blue bag was applied to the stings on my legs.

A week later a large owl was found sitting on the tailboard of one of the spare room beds. There was a plumber repairing a tap in the kitchen

Whippendell House, Chipperfield, Herts.
September 1931 to September 1934.

and he volunteered to remove the owl. The silly man didn't listen to my mother, who suggested he should throw his jacket over the bird before trying to pick it up, so it bit him badly. The owl was left where it was and he was rushed to hospital. That evening the windows were opened wide and in the dark it flew out.

Finally, there was my first encounter with a bat. Kiwi was taken upstairs to my parent's bedroom to see if he could either catch it, or frighten it enough so that it would fly out of the window. He leapt round after it and finally swiped it with his paw. The bat fell to the floor, folded its wings about its body and lay stock still, flat on its back. Kiwi sniffed it carefully, decided it wasn't a bird and therefore of no interest to him, and went and sat by the door. My mother had never seen a bat at close quarters, and assuming it was dead, bent down to take a good look. At that moment the bat took off, missing my mother by no more than a whisker and frightening the life out of her. Luckily this time it headed in the direction of the windows, which were wide open, and, encouraged by Kiwi leaping after it, shot out into the night.

In November we were joined by an Old English mastiff puppy. He was six months old, huge, all legs and paws. My mother could only just lift him. He was a present from a friend who bred mastiffs and thought we needed a guard dog! The puppy was named Cosmo, after its father, and he proved to be one of the most wonderful dogs I have ever known, and deserves a book just about him. Unfortunately we had already bought a wire-haired terrier, called Tigger because he was so bouncy, who led Cosmo astray. We had six-foot-high wire netting all round the garden. Tigger would dig a hole under it; Cosmo would put his nose through, give one good heave and rip up the netting. We had to change quickly to chain-link fencing, all pegged down.

In the spring my mother decided she would keep hens. She bought a dozen Light Sussex hens and a Rhode Island Red cockerel. We were going to hatch our own chickens and the Sussex crossed with a Rhode Island produced very good laying hens and nice table birds. Until then, procreation had not been a subject that bothered me very much. I knew where babies came from but had never been concerned with the mechanics of how they got there. I knew there was a difference between boys and girls because I had a younger brother.

His arrival had caused consternation on two counts. First, I had asked for a girl and was furious that someone had made a mistake. Second, I was so amazed to see what my baby brother looked like that for days the flat was littered with graphic drawings of one portion of his anatomy, and my mother suffered agonies as she went round collecting my artistic impressions. She decided it was best not to chastise me in case it only made me worse. So she pretended to ignore it all, hoping I would soon get tired and turn to something else. I have never been able to draw with any accuracy but, according to my mother, I was spot on with that subject. Eventually the novelty wore off and peace returned to the household. I never did learn what our nanny thought, but I bet Mum had a struggle to prevent her from saying something.

Christmas 1926 found my maternal grandparents paying their yearly visit to London. My brother was seven weeks old. We had the usual large family party with all the uncles, aunts and cousins who could easily reach London. My grandfather could draw exquisitely and he was always hoping that perhaps one grandchild would inherit his talent. After tea he asked me if I would care to draw something for him. My mother told me years later that she went pale with fear. This was dangerous territory – what would I be likely to draw? She was wondering what on earth to do when, fortunately, there was a complete diversion. Kiwi had managed to get into the kitchen during an unguarded moment and had the turkey carcass on the floor. I was told to take Kiwi to my father's study and leave him there until everyone had gone. When I returned one of my cousins was doing a drawing for Grandfather. The danger had been averted.

With hens and a cockerel the mysteries of life were revealed and my mother, once again, suffered agonies. I spent hours sitting in the hen run

The hens at Whippendell House.

watching our cockerel. Every time a hen laid an egg and began to cackle he would come belting along to mate it. I would count the number of times he performed and report back to my mother. It didn't matter where she was or whom she was with. I was a tiresome child, always saying the wrong thing at the most awkward moment. My poor mother again hoped the novelty would wear off, but she was finally stung into action when my grandparents were visiting us for a week during the summer of 1932. My grandfather asked me what I had been doing in the garden. "I have been watching our cockerel mating the hens and he does it awfully well," I replied with much enthusiasm. My mother paled, my grandmother looked stern and I was ordered to go to the playroom. There was something about the presence of my grandparents which made me obey immediately instead of asking what I had done. A few minutes later my mother joined me. I then discovered that sex was taboo because it embarrassed the adults and I had to promise not to mention the subject of the cockerel again, and, surprisingly enough, I didn't.

Just before we left London my father bought a second-hand 1926 Sunbeam Talbot. He loved the car and used any excuse to take us out. We even had a picnic on John's fifth birthday in November. It was very cold but we were used to open cars and were wrapped up to the eyebrows. Every weekend we would explore Hertfordshire and Buckinghamshire and came to know a considerable amount about both counties. It was during one of our excursions into deepest Bucks that my father invented his Aunt Matilda. He told us that she had been jilted by an architect when she was eighteen years old and it had affected her in a most astonishing way. She began building houses using Lotts Bricks and spit.

Lotts Bricks were beautifully made toy bricks, which were the craze during the 1920s and '30s, and we had a set of them. They were large enough to need no sticking together, came in several sizes and shapes, and two colours: shiny red and shiny fawn. Aunt Matilda chose the shiny red bricks for all the houses and shops she built.

My father couldn't bear the mass-produced small red shiny bricks. "One of Aunt Matilda's," he would say as we passed some awful red building. We took to looking for examples of Aunt Matilda's work wherever we went. As a result we noticed all the awful buildings and frequently missed the beautiful!

My father even sent us sketches of Aunt Matilda's excesses when he was away on business in some other part of the country. Once we received a sketch of a chapel he had seen in Wales. Here she had excelled herself and done some decorations on both sides of the porch door. The caption to the sketch read "Vines, done in cement", and underneath he had written "I never knew she got as far as Wales".

We felt very sorry for Aunt Matilda. She had a hard life and when she died, sometime during the 1950s, my father said producing all that spit had been a superhuman feat and had contributed to her death. She ran dry!

Kiwi took to country life far better than we had expected. Grass and trees he knew nothing about. In London his playground had been the flat roof outside my father's study, so to begin with he wouldn't venture very far away from the back door and it took him quite a while to give up using his earth tray, which had been put in the scullery. He was not very friendly with Cosmo and Tigger, or the stray cats that adopted us. The kitchen remained his territory: it had been so in London and he was not going to change his ways.

In London he had been a most loving and patient cat, even allowing me to dress him in my doll's clothes and put him in the doll's pram. When we moved all that changed. He was still a friendly cat, but far more on his guard. Life was different and dangerous and there were many new experiences to be learnt. After about six months he took to disappearing for a few days at a time, returning home scratched, bitten and ravenous. He would sleep for days on one of the beds, only coming downstairs to eat and have a run outside. Then, when he was sleek and well fed again, off he would go for another adventure. The adventures became longer and longer, sometimes up to a fortnight, and a very scruffy cat would suddenly return. He was so happy to be home again, fussing over us all and taking quite a while to recover. Once he returned with his tail nearly severed at the root. He had obviously been caught in a gin trap and someone had released him. Wearing my father's driving gauntlets I held Kiwi while the vet dressed his tail. Though it must have been agony and the poor cat growled and howled while his tail was being dealt with, he never tried to bite me. During his absence one of the strays would occupy Kiwi's chair in the kitchen. It was interesting to watch the intruder slinking quietly away when Kiwi returned!

By the time Cosmo was a year old, in May 1932, he proved that he was going to be a very good guard dog. He had terrified several unsuspecting callers so my father had a notice made for the gate. "Beware, Guard Dog", it said. An electrician came and a bell was installed. No one took any notice.

The next victim was a postman delivering the new telephone directory. He opened the gate and started up the drive, whistling. I happened to be playing outside the front door. I heard a terrific bark from Cosmo and the next second he came round the side of the house, heading for the postman, who was still walking up the drive. I yelled at Cosmo to stop, but he would only obey my mother. He just shot me a look and galloped on. I ran after him and reached him just as he took a mighty leap at the unfortunate man. I flung my arms round Cosmo's neck and hung on to him, begging the postman to turn round and make for the gate, which he did, throwing the directory at Cosmo. That angered him and he followed the man with me sitting on his back. He was a very strong dog.

Outside the gate was the post office van, a Trojan, into which the man leapt, quickly slamming the door. But he had left the window down and Cosmo stuck his head in and barked furiously. He must have been deafened, the poor man! Of course the Trojan wouldn't start and I can remember hanging onto Cosmo and shrieking at the postman, "Do drive away. I can't hold on to this dog much longer." Fortunately my mother had heard the commotion and arrived on the scene. Cosmo followed her meekly back to the house and next day another notice was made. This one said "Mastiff dog loose in grounds" and people did take notice!

The hens were such a success that Mum decided to try a few geese. The main advantage would be their ability to consume vast quantities of grass. We had pictures of the geese turning the orchard into a beautifully well-mown area. Mum began with six geese and a gander. The gander lasted for a month. He proved to be a formidable enemy and in self-defence we ate him. Even my mother had reservations after the first week and I had very sore legs from the nips I had received from him. Cosmo, that big brave dog, was terrified of all the geese and no longer accompanied my mother when she went to feed the hens. If the orchard gate was accidentally left open the geese would be out, quick as a flash, because they preferred grazing the lawns to the tough grass in the orchard.

One goose sat on about ten eggs and hatched six. The other eggs were infertile but I didn't know that. I took one of them up to the back yard and knelt down, holding it between my knees. Then I tapped it gently with a stone. It exploded with some force, shooting a large stream of rotten egg up into the air and it all came down on my head. That was the day I learnt about infertile eggs. I was put in the bath and scrubbed from head to toe!

The six goslings were great fun and I played with them frequently. Poor things – they must have suffered, because I carried them about whenever I could. They had a peculiar soft floppy feeling and didn't struggle. One very hot afternoon the orchard gate was left open and the goslings waddled round to the front of the house. We had a very nice large porch with windows on both sides and a glass door, which was big enough to contain three wicker garden chairs and a table. During the summer the porch door was usually left open. The goslings, feeling hot, decided they would go inside. They sat down on the coconut matting and dozed in the pleasant surroundings. My mother came downstairs from an afternoon nap just as two of the goslings decided to walk into the hall and take a look round. Though she shooed them out as quickly as possible, they left grass-green droppings in the hall and all over the coconut matting. The hall carpet recovered from the ordeal. The coconut matting was never the same; it was downgraded and removed to the conservatory. The geese and goslings were sold to a local farmer and John was given a pet rabbit.

Ever since we had moved to Chipperfield I had been begging my father to put up a swing. I had a passion for swings and when we lived in London I was always pestering my mother to let me have a go on the ones in Kensington Gardens. She was very reluctant and if I was allowed to swing I had to wear my gloves, which were washed as soon as we got home. As a child in Birkenhead my mother had caught impetigo, from a tram, it was thought, and I think it was the memory of the discomfort which made her so fussy.

In our garden I could have a swing of my own, so I nagged my father relentlessly. He finally gave way and in the summer of 1932 a swing went up. My father never did anything by halves. He chose a tree with a very large strong branch, at least twelve feet from the ground. A good wooden seat was made and he bought some very thick rope. He and the gardener spent a Saturday morning lashing the rope to the branch and by afternoon I was swinging happily. It was a perfect swing, though it took quite a lot of pumping to set it going. Unfortunately neither the gardener nor my father had taken into account the effect of friction, and one day my beautiful swing broke. Luckily for me it happened while I was pumping it up and not when I was in full flight or I could have been hurled to the ground from quite a height. Sadly, the swing was not repaired. My mother had been quite sure I was going to break my neck and she insisted that the remains be dismantled.

It must have been during the summer of 1932 that we had a terrible weekend, the sort one never forgets. My father in those days was in advertising and he invited a prospective client, with his wife and daughter, for

The geese and goslings at Whippendell House.

the weekend. They arrived on the Friday evening and disaster set in from the start. Cosmo took an instant disliking to the daughter, a thin small nine-year-old waif of a child called Pamela. She was terrified of Cosmo and he had to be put in his kennel. When they were shown to their rooms the spider, who by now had been named Joseph, put in an appearance. Mother and daughter had the vapours and the spider was captured and taken down to the bottom of the orchard, and put up a tree. We none of us mentioned that he always came back. In the evening my father discovered that neither of his guests drank. They looked on with a certain amount of disapproval while my parents had their customary tipple. The evening was a glum affair. The child, called Pammie by her parents, did not want to play but wandered round the garden talking to herself and looking for fairies. She went to bed early because, according to her mother, she was not very strong. I had come to the conclusion that she was a bit barmy.

The next day was to be special. We were going out for a picnic. We all crammed into the Talbot – Mrs Cooper and Pammie in the front and Mr Cooper, my mother, John and me in the back. The picnic hamper was strapped to the luggage rack. We had a very good cook in those days who could produce the most beautiful picnics. Everything was perfectly prepared and perfectly presented, with the china and cutlery wrapped in tissue paper, and little napkins for each person. Only on this day cook was in a rage. Mrs Cooper had criticised the food the night before and that sealed our fate. We went to Bledlow Right, not a soul about; it was beautiful. The hamper was placed on the ground. A rug was spread out and a large cloth put on top of it. We waited as the hamper was opened... Disaster stared us in the face. Cook had wrapped the china and cutlery in newspaper and there were no little napkins. The meal was all right except there was not enough of it and nobody could think of anything to say. My mother apologised and said she couldn't understand what had taken cook, and Mrs Cooper asked, "Does she drink?" We went home quickly and Mum and cook had a few words.

As soon as we were home Cosmo, who had been able to have a run in the garden during our absence, was hastily stuffed into his kennel. There was a scream from upstairs as the spider reappeared and it was removed, again to the bottom of the garden. The strain was beginning to tell on my mother and she retired for a short rest. My father and Mr Cooper had a business discussion and John and I tried to entertain Pammie. She decided to go and look for more fairies. Late that afternoon Tigger, who was normally a well-behaved dog, ate half a toy seal, made of real seal skin, which belonged to Pammie. Mrs Cooper announced that the incident was bound to bring on one of Pammie's attacks, so she was put to bed. With the little girl out of the way Cosmo was allowed out and he sat in the porch during supper. After supper there was another upset. Cosmo, who was also a well-behaved dog, had eaten the last six pages of Mr Cooper's thriller. It ruined his evening. Pa offered to buy him another copy, but, as Mr Cooper said with considerable feeling, that meant he had to wait until Monday to know who committed the crime. He and his wife also went to bed early.

It was one of those occasions where you know the fates are against you and there is nothing you can do. Sunday morning dawned bright, clear and hot. One more day to go. My father flung open the bathroom window

Cosmo, 18 months old, at Whippendell House.

and looked down at Cosmo's kennel: a small hen house because he was so big, and called out, "Don't worry, he shall have the idiot child, he shall," and at that moment who should come round the corner...? Mr Cooper! My father froze. Had he heard? After breakfast, when the Coopers were safely in the drawing room with the Sunday papers, a test was done. My father, up in the bathroom, repeated what he had said and my mother came round the corner, as Mr Cooper had done, to see if she could hear. The evidence was inconclusive because my mother knew what to expect and thought she had heard it. So the next few hours were agonising for them. It was a relief when Mr Cooper announced they would go home that afternoon, and not the following morning, because dear Pammie was not very well. We said our polite goodbyes. They thanked us for inviting them, but the half-eaten seal and the ruined thriller plus all the other incidents stood between us. My father did not get the account.

Between September 1932 and December 1937 I was away at boarding school so I missed the move from Whippendell House to Tenements Farm in September 1934. The day was marred by the absence of Kiwi. He had chosen to go on one of his treks a week before the move was to take place. The fateful day arrived with no sign of our cat. For several weeks, until the new owners moved in, Pa stopped at the house on his way to and from Kings Langley Station and walked around looking for him. When the new owners moved in Pa asked them to ring us if they ever saw Kiwi. But they never did.

I arrived back for the Christmas holidays to discover that Kiwi had been missing for nearly three months. Mum had not told me because she knew how upset I would be. We never heard of him again and I feared he must have been caught once more in a gin trap and killed. I was miserable without him and only slightly comforted by the arrival of a stray cat, which was the very image of one of the strays we had three years before. However, there was a new dog to meet, which helped a bit. Mum had bought a mastiff bitch puppy called Neda.

We had moved from one end of Chipperfield to the other and were now the Bovingdon side of the village. Tenements Farm was a lovely house. Probably built about the middle of the seventeenth century, it had been modernised by the previous owners. It had a small cellar with an Elizabethan brick floor. The dairy and one of the front rooms had been combined to make a long lounge. The other front room had been extended by taking in the passage, which would have run from front door to back door in the original house. That became our dining room. The kitchen had been altered to make the hall and cloakroom, and where the back door had been there was the front door with a vestibule. A new kitchen had been built onto the side of the house, with two small bedrooms above. All the windows had been replaced by metal-framed ones, with leaded lights. They looked very nice, upkeep was easy and every window shut properly. They had also made use of the roof space and built two nice rooms with dormer windows. There were two bathrooms, very small but that didn't matter, and four lavatories, counting the outside one, which was a great improvement on the last house! The old staircase had gone and a new polished oak one took its place. Thin walls and no central heating made it a cold house and in spite of plenty of lagging we were in danger of freezing up during the winter. Fortunately there were the vital trigger points, which were easy to get at with a blowlamp, and I became good at thawing us out when necessary.

All but five acres of the farm's land had been sold but the barns remained, intact, and one had been converted into a cottage with a large garage. Tenements Farm was an idyllic place.

Having failed my School Certificate I was removed from school in December 1937, and sent to a "crammers" in January 1938. My heart wasn't in it and in 1939 I failed again. The war put paid to all my petty problems and landed us with ten young children, a teacher and her mother. They were housed in the cottage, and half the garage was partitioned off and made into a playroom with a huge old boiler fitted in one corner. During that time the car was kept in the big barn. I now found myself cooking for a family which had grown overnight from the four of us to sixteen; and working on a very tight budget.

The evacuees were with us for about nine or ten months and then, feeling that the war was not going to get any worse, the parents decided to take them back to London just in time for the Battle of Britain and the London blitz, but not before they had all unwittingly been responsible for an agonising hour and a quarter. One of those events that remains forever in the mind.

It happened on a pouring wet Thursday afternoon in March 1940, at 3.45 pm to be precise. The front gate bell rang long and loud. I was in the kitchen doing a terrific turnout of the larder and all the kitchen cupboards. Our daily help, Mrs Gilbert, who normally worked from 9 am to noon, had come back to give me a helping hand. We looked at the bell indicator and then at one another. "FRONT" was waggling furiously. Who could be out there at this hour and in the pouring rain?

Tenements Farm, Chipperfield, Herts. September 1934 to April 1951.
Front of house from big cherry tree. Yard and open barn on right.

Cosmo was in the hall, deafening us with his barking, so I let him out through the front door. He tore round to the back of the house, convinced there was someone at the back gate. Our front gate, known euphemistically as the "hole in the wall" was hardly ever used. Its bell was temperamental and people had long ago discovered that if you wanted to announce your presence, the bell at the back gate, by the barn, was the one to try.

Neda, who had been sitting in the open barn, had already galloped to the back gate and on finding no one there had turned back and was tearing round to the front of the house to find out what was going on. The two dogs met, in a head-on collision, at the corner of the house. Each weighed about twelve stone and the crash was monumental. Cosmo, in his frustration and fury, bit Neda, not very badly. She, the most self-effacing and timid of wives, in her amazement bit him back, painfully on the lip. A row developed between them and I rushed out and shut all yard gates. Let us at least get the dogs under control.

The bell rang again. The dogs forgot their marital battle and resumed their barking. The noise was deafening. My awkward aunt was staying with us. She had been reading in the lounge and arrived in the kitchen as I returned from sorting out Cosmo and Neda. She felt someone ought to find out who was ringing the bell so urgently. At that moment Phillips, the gardener, stuck his head round the kitchen door and volunteered to go to the front gate. He was wearing a slit grain sack as a hood to keep the rain out and there was a faint but noticeable smell of hen manure. Also he had left his false teeth at home and was somewhat incoherent.

The bell rang for a third time so I readily accepted his offer. In a minute or two he was back, bearing a visiting card with the top right-hand corner turned down.

"Mrs Brown's chauffeur gave me this. He was grinning all over his face," reported Phillips.

My mother, who had been woken from her forty winks by the dogs, arrived downstairs at that moment to find my awkward aunt, Mrs Gilbert our daily help, Phillips and me, all staring at the visiting card. I had never had to deal with the etiquette of card leaving. The afternoon "at homes" and other such social happenings had largely died out after the First World War, though there were still some people who were loath to see old customs vanish. We were confronted by just such a person in Mrs Brown, whose card Mum now held.

"Why is the corner turned down?!" I asked.

"I can't remember," said Mum, frantically thinking back at least twenty-seven years, when as a girl she had to accompany her mother when she paid her social calls on friends, neighbours and acquaintances.

My awkward aunt was twittering away, saying it must mean something and her dear mama would be able to tell us. She would indeed but a phone call to Grandmama in Bolton was out of the question at that moment. Mrs Brown must have been outside for at least ten minutes and we really couldn't delay a moment longer. My mother looked at the card again… If only she could remember why one turned down the right-hand corner.

"I wonder if she is still there," I said and dashed up to the top of the house, because from a dormer window I would be able to see over the wall a bit, and, unless it was parked close in, a car would just be visible. Yes… I could just see the bonnet of a Daimler. Oh…! Heck, she was definitely calling on us. I rushed downstairs.

"The car is still there. She is definitely calling on us," I said.

"Shall I let her in?" asked Phillips. It was still pouring with rain.

"Where is the umbrella?" asked my aunt.

"Go and tell her we are just finding an umbrella," said Mum, and Phillips left to do her bidding, still with the sack draped over him.

The dogs, on observing the renewed activity, began barking again. They were sure someone was about to be let in. From the yard they could see the "hole in the wall". I began hunting for an umbrella. Oh!

Exasperation. Where on earth was it? I tried the cloakroom, nothing there; the box room, nothing there; and my mother's wardrobe, another blank.

"Mum," I yelled as I tore downstairs, "I can't find it anywhere."

"There is only one thing for it – a raincoat held over her," replied Mum and she fetched an old one of Pa's from the cloakroom.

"Put a kettle on quickly," she said, turning to me. "We'll have to give her a cup of tea."

"But we've got nothing to eat," I wailed. We didn't have afternoon tea except on special occasions.

"Shortbread," said my aunt. "I'm sure there's some shortbread." This was quickly becoming one of those situations one could well have done without.

I went back to the kitchen to see what could be done. Mrs Gilbert had returned to the job in hand and in the mounting chaos I tried to find enough of the tea set for three people. The silver teapot needed polishing so I couldn't use it. There was nowhere to put a tray and a feeling of gentle panic began to grip me. Shortbread? Where on earth was it? I finally found the tin under the kitchen table. Just two slices remained. Oh dear, that would look lonely. No biscuits, no cake, nothing. Friday was our main shopping and baking day. Thursday was always bleak! Ah, sandwiches, that was a good idea. No it wasn't: there was only the tail end of a stale white loaf – just enough for the three of us to have with our eggs at breakfast – and one large tomato. Clearing a corner of the table, just enough to take the breadboard, I made two rounds of very thin tomato sandwiches. Cut into quarters and arranged on a very small plate they looked presentable though a bit meagre.

Meanwhile my mother was suffering agonies. She tended at times to put her foot in it, particularly if the going was hard. Accompanied by Phillips holding the raincoat over her as best he could, Mrs Brown had made her way up the path to the front door. There she had to negotiate an enormous puddle, which Phillips steered her round with care. She was most unsuitably dressed in a fur coat, high-heeled shoes and a hat with what my mother, in the agony of the moment, thought was a large bunch of pheasant's feathers standing straight up on one side. Only some time later did she realise it was half a bird of paradise, but by then it was too late.

Mrs Brown stepped into the vestibule. My mother greeted her with a smile and the friendly words, "I do hope you can swim," before remembering that Mrs Brown regarded herself as a swimmer of some note and had been known to give demonstrations. Mrs Brown snorted. "And," continued my mother, driven on by some unseen and obviously uncaring force, "Do mind those pheasant's feathers on that ham," and she indicated a huge leg of ham with the word CANADA stamped on it, which hung from a convenient beam. Mrs Brown stared at it and then at Mum.

"Present from a friend who thinks we are starving," informed my mother gaily. My aunt was introduced.

"Oh, so sorry we couldn't find an umbrella," twittered that worthy relative. "Madge has dozens of them – don't you, Madge – we just couldn't find any of them," she giggled. Mum could have strangled her.

The next problem was tea. If Mum rang the bell the chances were that I would answer it, still dressed in my brother's old school trousers, which always caused an argument because a fly opening was unladylike; an old sweater, socks and sandals. Or worse still it might be Phillips! Also the dogs were quiet and if a bell rang they would start barking again. So my mother played it safe and asked my aunt to see if tea was ready.

"I do hope, Mrs Brown," twittered my aunt when she returned with the tea tray, "that you are not hungry." She had her own way of putting her foot in it. Mrs Brown got her own back.

"Oh, how kind," she said and ate all the sandwiches. My aunt didn't get over it for days!

It transpired that Mrs Brown was on the local committee for the wellbeing of evacuees, or some such body, and was visiting to enquire if ours were all right.

"No problems or anything, dear lady?" she enquired. Mum assured her that all was well and offered to take her to the cottage, where they were happily ensconced.

"No need. I shall take your word for it," replied Mrs Brown.

The rain had stopped by the time she took her leave. My mother and aunt accompanied her to the gate. The chauffeur caught Mum's eye as he held open the car door, and grinned from ear to ear.

Back in the house Mum sat down, worn out from the effort of trying to keep my awkward aunt quiet and at the same time talk to Mrs Brown. That visiting card with its turned-down corner mocked her from the small table on which it lay. Pa at once bought a book on etiquette and we read it avidly. Mrs Brown had turned down the corner because she left the card personally (in other words she was outside waiting to see if Mum was at home) but she had sent the card by a servant (her chauffeur) because the call was of a business nature and she and my mother had never met before.

It was a pity we none of us thought of sending a message back to say Mum was out. However, it provided us with a good laugh, when we had recovered, and the following weekend when some friends of ours called they left behind a book of matches with the right-hand corner turned down.

A month or two after the evacuees had left we received an unexpected visit from two men who were looking for suitable temporary storage space for tins of emergency rations. All her life my mother had had a suspicion that the officials who were appointed to look after our wellbeing were wasting their time and could find much more worthwhile work, if only they looked for it. She said as much to an inspector of taxes during the First World War and he was most upset! The two men were in their early thirties and explained that they were in a reserved occupation, when questioned as to why they had not been called up.

"I understand," said one of them, "that your large garage is empty, now that the evacuees have gone."

"How do you know all that?" asked Mum, whereupon documents were produced which, to her surprise, gave detailed information about all the accommodation we had. It had all come from the officials who had dealt with the billeting of evacuees. So my mother showed them the garage and promptly found herself responsible for receiving tins of biscuits, which would be delivered shortly. It meant padlocks on the main garage doors and on the back door to the garage. It was made plain to Mum that she would be responsible for the safety of the emergency rations.

Two days later a huge lorry arrived and began unloading the tins. We went out to make sure everything was done properly and found the same young men were in charge.

"Just a minute," said Mum as the first half-dozen tins were carried into the garage. "I will be counting them all."

"ALL of them?" echoed the first young man, in disbelief.

"All of them," repeated my mother. "You have made it quite plain that I am responsible for every tin and I want to be sure that the correct number has arrived." The men look aghast. This would slow down the unloading considerably.

"But we have another three calls to make today," one of them protested.

"In that case you had better not unload these here," replied my mother. Mum stood erect, all five foot two inches of her, and the men knew they were beaten.

They began unloading and Mum noted down every tin that went in, totted them up at the end, pronounced herself satisfied that the correct number had been delivered and signed the necessary papers. In triplicate.

Before the end of 1940 the men were back to collect the biscuits. Permanent storage places had now been requisitioned, or built. It was a different four this time. The man in charge was a cheeky individual.

"I have come to collect the tins of biscuits. Where are the keys to the garage?"

"Where is your authority?" asked my mother.

"In the lorry," he replied, looking insolently at Mum.

"Show it to me, or you do not take the biscuits." He looked at her and quickly realised he was beaten. She read through the authorisation, checked that the number of tins tallied with the number she had signed for, and asked me to fetch the keys. The men began loading the lorry.

"I am counting the tins as you remove them," said Mum to the man in charge.

"Oh, God!" he said, and opened his mouth to say something more, thought better of it, and instructed the men to let Mum count the tins.

Suddenly there was a shout from the same man. "Look here," he called from the middle of the pile of tins in the garage, "You've opened one of them. All the biscuits have gone; it's empty," and he waved the empty tin under Mum's nose.

Mum was unmoved. "Oh yes," she said. "We would be likely to remove all the top tins to reach one at the bottom, open it, take out the biscuits and replace all the full tins on top of it. Tell me," she continued, "how did we open the tin?" The man turned it round and examined it carefully. Then he looked accusingly at Mum. "It's not been opened. So what's happened?"

"Ever heard of mice?" enquired my mother. "Have a look for a very small hole." He turned it round again and there, in one corner, was a small hole.

"Good heavens," he said. "These are tins with double skins and they have eaten through both. What am I to put on this form?"

Mum came to his rescue. "I shall put on the form, 'one tin eaten by mice', and we shall both sign it. Then show them the tin and it will be all right." The loading was finished, the forms signed and with a sigh of relief we said goodbye to hundreds of tins of emergency ration biscuits. The next officials to call on us were men from the Ministry of Agriculture, but that wasn't until much later on.

After the evacuees had gone, we all agreed that we ought to make the most of our five acres and decided to run a smallholding. My mother, who was not in the best of health, was sure she could manage to keep rabbits, to help the meat ration. The work, though time-consuming, would not be heavy. She began with four does and a buck, but after a few months they were increased to twelve does and two bucks and, to the delight of the local butcher, a thriving small industry was born.

Fortunately Phillips was not called up until late 1943, so we had his help while we were trying to plan our smallholding. He had been with us since 1934 and lived in Croxley Green. He cycled to work each day, and like all good countrymen, he was versatile and enterprising. He was also very observant and it was amazing the things he noticed on his way to and from work. Once it was a canary in a tree, but he couldn't catch it, so someone's pet must finally have died. Then he saw a tame rabbit loping along, which he did manage to catch and he took it home for his children. But the best occasion was when he arrived one morning towing about a mile of telephone wire behind him. He had noticed the wire lying at the side of the road, so he cycled on to see if the other end was attached to the telegraph pole. It wasn't, so we had a roll of copper wire, which came in very handy and lasted for ages.

In the summer of 1940 an Airspeed Oxford, on a training flight, made a forced landing in a wheat field further down the lane. We all rushed down to see it. Fortunately no one was hurt and the aeroplane did not burst into flames. When it was finally collected they were amazed at how little petrol remained! So, when a few years later a Spitfire on a training flight made an emergency landing in another field, the Home Guard were immediately asked to guard it until the Army could take over. I had dashed down on hearing the incredible tin-can-bashing sound as, wheels up, the Spitfire had hopped over a hedge. The pilot was not in the plane: he had gone to the nearest house to report his landing. I was gazing into the cockpit when the first Home Guard arrived, not in uniform but with his rifle. He wanted to know what I was doing there and told me to go home. The army, he reassured me, would take over the guard duty. He was right: they did, at midnight.

The ringing of the bell and the barking of Cosmo, who always slept in the hall on an enormous dog's bed, woke mum and me. I went down to see which indicator was waggling. It was the front gate again. Back upstairs Mum decided to shout from a window of the spare bedroom, which was opposite the wall.

"Hallo," she yelled, "who is there?" Cosmo started barking again so the reply was difficult to hear.

"It's the..." woof...woof...woof... "...telephone, please?" On hearing the word "telephone" Mum replied, "Try the cottage, please." By now the two men had stepped back from the gate and we could just see them in the moonlight.

"We have..." woof ...woof ...woof ... "... of order." This was getting us nowhere and I rushed downstairs and shut Cosmo in the kitchen.

When I returned Mum was asking for name, rank and number, please. I decided not to point out that we wouldn't recognise them if he gave them to us. However, he obliged and, fortunately, said he came from the unit in Watford, which we did know about. "It's about the Spitfire," he yelled.

In our dressing-gowns and clutching a feeble torch we went to escort them to the house.

"I apologise for the delay," said Mum when we were in the house. "My daughter and I are here alone and because of the war one has to be careful." The captain nodded sympathetically and I caught the eye of the young lieutenant, who was desperately trying not to laugh. Cosmo began barking again and was pounding on the kitchen door with a paw. "It sounds like a very big dog in there," he said.

"It is," agreed my mother. "An Old English mastiff, an excellent guard dog." And she led them to the telephone.

The captain made his telephone call, received his orders and we escorted them to the gate.

Then I noticed a jeep parked close to the wall, containing more soldiers. What they made of all the yelling, goodness only knows.

That unit in Watford became one of the holding units for the D-Day build-up and at one stage Peter Hanscomb was its adjutant. He had a few tricky moments when a whole lot of Newfoundlanders arrived there and immediately demanded to know where the Americans were, because they wanted to knock seven bells out of them. They were hastily moved to another depot!

My mother was definitely an animal lover and my father definitely was not. His business was in London and when petrol was rationed he gave up commuting from Kings Langley Station and spent four nights in London and three nights at home. In London he was an air raid warden and at weekends he was busy with the local Home Guard. He applauded our efforts to set up our smallholding, providing we did not expect him to become very involved. So we agreed that he would shell out the money and we would do the work! Though in all fairness, I must add that he did help with collecting rabbit food at weekends. When driving to and from the various Home Guard meetings, parades and exercises, he kept his eyes open for any suitable rabbit food growing by the roadside. He had a sack in the boot of the car and sometimes managed to fill it to the top. But that was as far as it went; so when a friend of ours suggested we should buy some sheep to graze the grass in the orchard, as a start to our improvement plan, we wondered what Pa would think. He finally agreed to our request and six ewes arrived. They certainly ate the grass. They also got out and ate many other things as well. It was some time before we got the measure of our flock. Due to my total ignorance the six ewes turned out to be four. The other two were wethers (castrated rams), which didn't really matter, as we only wanted them to eat the grass. But it taught me a lesson, and in future I tried to be a bit more careful and a little less trusting!

My twenty-first birthday present that year was a beautiful pedigree Guernsey cow, whose registered name was "Rose of Stocks Hotel". She was Guernsey born and bred. Her milk would be useful for fattening cockerels and I thought I might fatten bull calves to send to market. Rose turned out to be a cow with a character. All cows are inquisitive; Rose was exceptionally so. I had expected her to miss the herd, but not a bit of it – she settled in as though being a lone cow was nothing out of the ordinary. The herd she came from had not been kept in at night, except when the weather was very cold, and I continued the practice.

Cosmo and Neda were horrified to find a cow had joined us. A year or two earlier Cosmo had been chased by a black cow which Miss Hawes, a neighbouring farmer, had asked if she may put into our field for a few months. We had all stood by the fence, holding up the bottom strand of barbed wire, which was rather slack, shouting encouraging words to Cosmo. Not one of us had the courage to go into the field to ward off the cow. She was a formidable beast so poor Cosmo was on his own. He only just made it. He was then eight years old and suffering from rheumatism in his hind legs.

Rose was introduced to him in the yard. He stood looking at her for a moment before turning round swiftly and rushing into the house. But not before shooting a look at Mum which plainly said, "We aren't having one of those, are we?" Neda was a highly strung animal anyhow and regarded Rose and the sheep as dangerous. She kept well away from them all.

At last the plans for our smallholding were taking shape and we managed to keep it running, relatively smoothly, until the autumn of 1946.

Back of house taken from Cottage roof, showing kitchen extension, open barn and yard with the arbour where we penned the sheep for dipping.

Chapter Two

Once we had established a good routine on our smallholding I decided to join the local branch of the Women's Land Army. After dealing with my livestock in the morning I wasn't really needed until late afternoon for the milking of Rose and the feeding of the sheep and calves.

So, early in 1941 I visited the Labour Exchange in Hemel Hempstead to make my enquiries. I discovered I was barred from joining because we were running a smallholding and I was classified as a farmer's daughter. The alternative was to find out if any of the local farmers needed help, and that is how I came to be working with Frank Pritchard and his sons Jim and Georgie.

I presented myself for work one Monday in April, wearing a school shirt and sweater that were too small for John; a new bib and brace; and a pair of good stout boots which I had managed to find in Watford.

The first thing I had to do was learn how to harness a horse. Jim was my instructor. He passed me an enormous collar and told me to put it over the horse's head.

"Does he bite?" I asked anxiously.

"Not this one," said Jim.

At that moment the horse, called Dick, yawned and showed a formidable set of teeth. I moved back a step.

"It must be similar to being attacked by a pair of pincers," I said, wondering if my idea of going to work on a farm was, after all, the right one.

Frank owned about forty acres at Tuffs Farm, which was only a minute or two from us. He grew mainly cereals, root crops and hay, and the rest of the time was spent doing contract work for neighbouring farmers. My first jobs were the usual ones: mucking out the stables, the cowshed, and the pigsty when there were any pigs. I also prepared the feed for all the animals and did any general tasks needing doing. My timetable was fairly tight. I had to attend to my livestock first thing in the morning: milking the cow, feeding any calves we had, mucking out the cowshed, dealing with the sheep, making sure all the animals had sufficient water for the day, generally leaving everything ready for the evening. I worked from 9 am to 5 pm and then went home to do the milking and attend to my livestock.

I did not work at the farm over the weekends, which gave me time to catch up with jobs at home. It was hard work but I loved every minute of it.

I often helped with harnessing the horses and I groomed them from time to time, but my first attempt at horsemanship was driving an old pony called Dolly, when haymaking began in early July. I had successfully harnessed her by myself and even put her in the hayrake, so I was feeling pretty pleased. Harnessing a horse is not difficult with a cooperative animal. The collar goes over the head, upside down and then turned round so the wide part is resting on the shoulders and the narrow part on the withers (where the mane ends). Then the hames are put on the collar, from which hang the traces. These are thick, long lengths of leather with chains at the end, and are attached to whatever the horse is going to pull. Next, there is the saddle, and the design depends on whether the horse is ploughing or working between shafts.

The hayrake was a large clattering contraption on two wheels. Between the wheels were carved tines, which just touched the ground and picked up the hay. When the rake was full you had to tread on a foot pedal or pull the lever, which raised the tines and deposited the hay in a neat long sausage. The idea was to go backwards and forwards across the field, leaving nice straight rows of hay ready for the sweeps.

Sweeps were huge wooden combs with broad flat teeth, to which a horse was harnessed. The teeth ran along the ground, picking up the hay. There were two handles at the back end so the driver could guide the sweep and thus take the hay to the stack.

Dolly was about twenty years old, a bit broken-winded (horse's emphysema) and slow. She was a gentle animal and excellent for a beginner. Not being dim – no animals are – she knew she had a learner the other end of the reins, so she was slower than ever. Frequent stops occurred.

"Just getting my breath back," she would signal with her ears, and she was deaf to my pleadings to get a move on.

"I'll cut you a little stick," my boss said. "You touch her with that, she'll move." She didn't, but when she saw Jim looming up she decided discretion was the better part of valour and resumed work. Dolly and I did quite a lot of hay raking together that year.

Those were the days of mostly unmechanised farming in our corner of Hertfordshire. Frank did all his work with horses. There were a few tractors on the bigger farms, which were used for ploughing, harrowing and rolling, but those farms had horses for all the other jobs. I remember watching a David Brown tractor, bright red in colour, being driven in top

My red setter Goldielocks and Neda.

gear over a field which was to be sown with winter wheat. It was towing a ring roller at such a speed that, at times, the roller bounced off the ground and came down with a resounding clang. "Well," I thought, in all my wisdom of a few months on a farm, "if that is rolling with a tractor, give me a horse any day." It did not occur to me then that a lower gear and less speed was the simple answer!

Life was good. I was blissfully happy, painfully sunburnt on my knees through stupidly wearing a pair of shorts when driving the hayrake one boiling hot day, but otherwise in my element. My first attempt at driving a horse on the road was embarrassing from start to finish. I had to fetch a load of old potatoes and was told to take a very quiet mare called Kitty. I knew all about harnessing by now and Kitty was a most helpful horse. She put her head down so I could slip the collar on easily. She opened her mouth for the bit when I put the bridle on, and getting her between the shafts of the cart presented no problems. Full of confidence, I drove out of the yard and turned left. I was a bit surprised to notice that Kitty had begun to turn left before I pulled on the rein, but I didn't attach any significance to it. We had gone about a hundred yards when Kitty turned left again, down the little lane that ran alongside Frank's fields.

"No, Kitty," I said, as I frantically pulled on the reins. "Whoa, you silly mare." Kitty came to an abrupt stop. This was awkward; I would have to back her out onto the road. Fortunately there was not much traffic about in those days so I could take my time, which was just as well because I couldn't budge her to begin with. In desperation I grabbed both reins in my right hand, under her jaw, and pushed against her mouth with all my strength.

Reluctantly and very slowly, Kitty backed out into the road. I led her forward a few yards so that we were past the lane, and climbed on board.

"Gee up, Kitty," I said, slapping the reins on her back. She went about fifty yards and stopped abruptly. This was becoming embarrassing. What on earth was the matter? I hopped down again and decided to lead her for a bit, to see if she was willing to walk at all! There was no problem: she walked on quite happily. So back I climbed and sure enough, she stopped again. Oh, blast! I was going to have to walk – there was no other way, or we would never get there.

I reached my destination, loaded up the potatoes and climbed on board to see if Kitty would behave which she did, perfectly. The potatoes were delivered to the address I had been given and Kitty and I headed for home. No problems on the way back – she walked on just like any sensible horse. We were about one hundred yards from home, when Kitty, without any warning whatever, abruptly turned right, towards that wretched lane again.

"Kitty," I yelled. "Not that way," and I hauled frantically on the left rein to pull her back. She responded slowly and reluctantly and a car, which had come up behind me, honked impatiently.

We reached the yard and Frank came out of the house.

"You got back safely, I see," he said. I told him about Kitty. He roared with laughter.

"She does 'night cart' work once a week," he told me. "She would want to go down that lane because that's where the chap empties the tank. Where she stopped up the road will be outside one of the cottages he goes to." I looked at Kitty. Stupid horse, she did lots of other work.

"Why should she choose to remember the night cart round?" I said. Frank laughed again.

"They're not fools; they know when they can play up a bit!"

The night cart was a large cylindrical tank on wheels, with a lid. One night a week a council employee went round emptying the earth closets which were in the back gardens of a row of cottages, a little way up the road from Frank's farm. The effluent was emptied in Frank's top field; alongside one of the hedges. In summer the smell was powerful, the flies numerous; and one year the wheat he grew in that field was nearly six feet high beside that hedge.

When harvest time came round I was introduced to the art of stooking, or shocking, depending on which part of the country you came from. First the corn (oats, barley or wheat) had to be reaped, using a string binder, a horse drawn machine, which cut the corn, then bundled it into sheaves and tied it with string. The first job was to "open the field" which was done by cutting "roads" round the outside of it, using a scythe. The cut corn was bundled together in sheaves and tied by hand, using several lengths of straw wrapped round each sheaf. The ends were then twisted together and tucked under the band. Jim used to scythe round the field and on several occasions I was the unlucky one who was following him and making up the sheaves. Unlucky, because it was round the edge of a cornfield that the best and biggest of the thistles grew – tall, healthy, and incredibly prickly. It didn't matter what shirt and gloves I wore – the thistles always managed to get me, and my arms were red and sore by the end of that job.

After the road had been cut the binder would begin reaping. It was driven round the field, finishing in the middle. Our job was to follow it, picking up the sheaves. Six sheaves to a stook was the usual number. They stood on their butt ends with their heads together as in a letter A. This was so that the sun and wind could dry them, before they were carted off the field to be either stacked outside and then thatched, or stacked in a barn. Just occasionally the cereal was threshed from the stooks.

In the winter the threshing tackle went round the local farms and each day we would go along to help. In the intervening years I had tended to forget about steam, so you can imagine my joy when I arrived for work one day to be told we were to go threshing! I hopped back on my bicycle and shot off to Percy's farm, which was about a mile away. As I pedalled into the yard I could see the smoke drifting over the barn roof. I dashed found the corner and there it was, a general-purpose Fowler No11362, hitched up to a threshing drum and a trusser. One of Percy's men came over to me as I stood gawping at the engine.

"Well, I never would have believed it!" he said, by way of introduction. "I was told Frank had a girl working for him, but I never would have believed it," and he shook his head. "Have you done any of this before?" he asked.

"'Fraid not," I replied, quite unable to take my eyes off that engine. She was gently rocking to the rhythm of the piston. Two men were going round the threshing drum, or box as it was sometimes called, checking that all was in order. There were little squeaky noises coming from it and dozens of belts were driving all the assorted mechanisms. I stood rooted to the spot. Somehow I couldn't believe it all.

"Well, you had better begin by removing the cavings from underneath the drum and piling it over there," and he waved his pitchfork in the general direction of an old tree. I was handed a short-handled pitchfork, a thin-tined fork and a bushel basket.

"It's awkward stuff to handle, being so light and dusty," I was told, "but do your best to keep the underneath of the drum clear of it."

I waited for the threshing to begin. Jim was there, clipping sacks in place, ready to receive the wheat as it came out of the drum. Soon everything was set up and we were ready to start. Didi Hobbs was up on top. He was the feeder and as each sheaf was passed to him he deftly cut the string and fed the sheaf into the drum. The note of the drum changed slightly as it began to work.

Didi soon got into his stride. The sheaves were being passed to him quickly and rhythmically and equally quickly he was feeding the drum, which had settled down to a continuous drone. Sometimes a bigger sheaf would be fed in and the traction engine would slow down a little. The drone of the drum would drop a note or two, then the Watt governor would open the throttle valve and the engine would pick up again with a characteristic "chuff – CHUFF, ER, CHUFF, ER, CHUFF, chuff" and be back to a steady rhythm again. Music to my ears. I loved it.

Threshing was an incredibly dusty job and when I arrived home that evening I itched from head to toe. Being a hay fever sufferer I was inclined to be allergic to dusty scratchy things and the cavings had managed to penetrate all the gaps in my clothing. My mother had to bathe my back with vinegar and water to stop the itching and I dabbed it over the rest of me. I was a sight for sore eyes. The next day I went in a polo-necked sweater, took a

The Cottage, which had been the cowshed until re-built in 1932.

headscarf as well as one to act as a mask, wore gloves, and tied string round the bottom of my trouser legs. Funnily enough I hardly ever had an attack of hay fever while haymaking, harvesting or threshing, but the minute I reached home I would begin to wheeze and my eyes would itch like mad. It seemed I was all right while I was busy. When we were threshing I hadn't time to sneeze. It was as much as I could do to keep up with the cavings. The drum had no blower to take it out at the side, as was the case with the more modern designs, so it piled up underneath. Cavings were the little bits that didn't go through with the corn or the straw and was mainly made up of the very thin outer leaf of the ear, dust, and weed seeds. It was light, flimsy and blew away easily. There was no use for the stuff at all except if the ground was very wet and then we used to spread it about and trample it into the mud. Trying to pick it up with a fork of any sort was rather like collecting water in a sieve!

I was delighted that steam had come back into my life, and for five winters I helped with the threshing on our local farms. That was my introduction to T T Boughton of Little Chalfont, who began work with just four threshing sets. Each set comprised a 54-foot drum, a trusser, an elevator for getting the trusses to the top of the stack, a baler and a chaff cutter. This was used when the farmer wanted the straw cut up for feed for the horses. It was mixed with the oat ration and provided bulk.

I was to learn much later that it was the single-cylinder general-purpose engine which dominated the threshing scene. Compound engines had arrived by 1881 but the single was regarded as better for this specific task. They could work all day on 80 psi (pounds per square inch) steam pressure whereas the compound needed at least 140 psi. It took longer to get a compound up to the required pressure, so the driver would have to be there very early in the morning. Also there were many more oiling points that needed attention during the day. A single-cylinder engine would burn five hundredweight of coal per day with the trusser attached, up to seven hundredweight with the baler and a bit more with the chaff cutter on. Chaff cutting made the engine work hard. Coal was nineteen shillings a ton, or 95p in present day money. The advantage with a compound was that it burnt less coal. The makers claimed a 25 per cent saving in fuel, but they were much more expensive to buy and more difficult to govern at low pressures.

One day I had to go ahead of the threshing tackle to be on site to explain to the driver, Bill, just where the drum was to be situated. We were aiming to start in the afternoon and hoping to complete the job the next day. We had about sixteen acres of wheat to thresh and at an acre an hour it would be done in a day and a half. Usually by the time I arrived in the morning they were already set up, so at last I would have a chance to watch it all.

The drum was parked alongside the rick and levelled by means of jacks fitted to it. There were also built-in spirit levels to ensure accuracy. If it wasn't level the corn would be going into the wrong sacks. Finally, the shutters were let down to provide the feeding platform. Meanwhile Bill was getting the engine in position and checking that it too was level with the driving pulleys of the drum. The main belt from the drum to the engine flywheel was hitched up. It turned out to be too slack and had to be removed so that the engine could be backed a bit. When all was finally in order the back wheels of the engine were chocked and a test run carried out. This meant setting the engine in action slowly, then building up to the operating speed, with little squeaks and noises coming from the drum as it ran unloaded.

It is hard to believe that the threshing drum was only in use for about a hundred years. Before that cereals were threshed using a flail. It is easy to understand how bread was not cheap until the advent of the string binder and the threshing drum. Before the days of the binder a gang of seven could harvest about two acres a day, using scythes. With a binder three or four men could harvest twelve to fourteen acres a day. With a flail eight bushels of wheat could be threshed in a day. With the drum sixty to eighty bushels an hour. A very great improvement.

Our four ewes had been to the ram in mid-November. The lambs would arrive mid-April, when the weather was likely to be less cold. Frank knew a farmer near Latimer who was willing for our ewes to join his flock for about four weeks. Phillips and I took them over in Frank's float one frosty morning and we thought the farmer would never stop laughing when he saw our sheep. The farmer was expecting a least a dozen. I cannot remember now what identification marks we put on ours, so that we could claim them when the time came. All four ewes were served by the ram, as the red on their rumps proved. In order to identify the sheep that had been served the ram had a dye put on his chest, which came off on the ewe's wool.

From the end of December the ewes' daily feed was increased. They had to be fed enough to put on a bit of weight – something in the order of twenty pounds – so that they could produce good healthy lambs. Mid-April arrived and three of the lambs were born when I was at work. The fourth chose four o'clock in the morning, and naturally, was the one that needed assistance. We had put the ewes in pens made out of hurdles, on the front lawn, where they would be out of the way of inquisitive dogs. The one which hadn't lambed was in a pen on her own. Her bleating woke me and I reluctantly struggled out of bed. I hadn't bothered to put up the blackout the night before, and hunting for suitable clothing in the pitch dark took ages. Grabbing a feeble torch we kept handy in the kitchen, I went out to look at the ewe. All the sheep had joined in by now and woken the whole house. Luckily neither of the mastiffs took any notice, which was just as well since we knew their barking would be heard for miles!

The ewe was straining to no effect, and the lamb's front hooves were plainly visible. I fetched a bucket of hot water, soap and a towel and returned to the pen. I had never helped any animal give birth to its young and I was somewhat apprehensive. John had joined me to see if he could help and I was grateful for his moral support. On occasions like that I found it very helpful to have someone to talk to! The sheep would not lie down, so John said he would hold her up while I lambed her. She was definitely in pain and I examined her to make sure the head was not twisted back. Everything was where it should have been but the lamb had a very big head and the ewe was small. There was only one thing for it: I would have to grab the lamb by the hooves and pull whenever the ewe strained. It took some time, but it worked and with a final heave from the ewe and a mighty tug from me, one large, wet, slippery lamb landed in my lap. John was mightily glad it was all over because the sheep had given up standing on its hind legs and John had been holding her up for a long time! I rubbed the lamb with the towel to help to dry it, as it was a very chilly morning. We were delighted with our handiwork and feeling very pleased, we staggered back to our beds. That was the only lamb I ever delivered.

Spring also saw the birth of Rose's calf. It was a bull: an Ayrshire–Guernsey cross. Fortunately we lived next door to a farm that had a large herd of pedigree, tuberculosis-free Ayrshires and Rose had been served by one of the bulls the previous August. I had not been very popular with her because three weeks after she had been served I thought she had come into season again. She was restless, mooing and wandering around the field aimlessly. So back to the bull she went. He was a beautiful animal, big, and to my surprise, quite easy to handle. I held Rose, while the bull was brought out of his pen. She didn't seem very pleased to see him, and began to walk out of the yard. I hauled her back and the bull approached her. Rose shook her head at him and he eyed her doubtfully. It hadn't been like this on her first visit. Then she had definitely been pleased to see him. The bull was manoeuvred up behind Rose, who was quite determined to avoid him at all costs. She took off over a pile of brushwood, which was lying in the middle of the yard, tripped and went down on her knees – only momentarily – but the bull wasn't slow and he seized the opportunity to mount her. "Pull her tail to one side, quickly," I was commanded. I hastily did as instructed and the bull mated her successfully. Rose let out a furious MOO-O-O-O-O, got to her feet, climbed off the brushwood, turned and rammed her horns into the unfortunate bull's ribs. He looked amazed and was removed to his shed. I grabbed hold of the rope from Rose's halter just in time to catch her as she set off at a smart trot out of the yard. She was not amused. She strode the short distance back home, mooing at intervals. I put her in the field and left one furious cow to calm down. She would not come in for milking at 5.30 and I had to fetch her. She was in a thoroughly bad temper and was several pints down on her usual output. When she had her calf it was born on the right date for the first mating. No wonder she had been so furious at being mated a second time. She had more than likely eaten something that had upset her so was feeling a bit off-colour, hence the mooing and restlessness. I was more careful the next time.

The bull calf was a big one, but instead of rearing it as a veal calf, I bought two week-old Ayrshire heifer calves and reared them until they were six months old. They were fed entirely on milk for the first eight weeks and then I introduced them to "Calf Starter", which was a milk substitute. This enabled me to reduce the amount of milk they were having. As soon as they had settled to the change in the feeding I added hay and chopped-up vegetables to their diet. They did very well so I bought two more week-old calves. It did mean that our milk had to be rationed for eight weeks, as the two older calves were still having a pint or two each. But it worked well and I was pleased with the way the calves thrived. Many years later I happened to read an article which warned against giving rich Channel Island milk to calves of breeds such as Ayrshire and Friesian. The milk would be too rich for them. I must have been lucky because it never seemed to do them any harm, and Rose's milk was rich.

My luck did not extend to the lambs and, sadly, they had all died. They had started off very well but then become sickly. A post mortem on the first one revealed a terrific infestation of strongyle worms. Its stomach was full of them and the vet held out little hope for the other three. It was, apparently, a bad year for worms, which the lambs would have picked up from the pasture. The only possible treatment was to dose them with arsenic worm tablets, but even those weren't all that effective. Phenothiazine was not on the market until a few years later. I was sorry to lose the lambs. I did enjoy watching them skipping round and chasing one another. For a few days after they were born we had left them penned on the lawn so the ewes would crop the grass nice and low. One lamb found it could just squeeze under a hurdle that had a bent bottom bar. It skipped round, eating Mum's daffodils and polyanthus, and was extremely difficult to catch.

By now I had been working on the farm for a year and at last I was sent on my own to some of the jobs to be done on other farms. One entailed chain harrowing about four acres of old pasture. I was given a six-year-old horse called Prince. He had an enormous stride and couldn't walk slowly. He was a jumpy horse: nothing must touch his heels or he would be away. While hitching him up to the chain harrow I had to be particularly careful, and as for turning him at the end of the field, that was no joke. Chain harrows could be turned over easily, which would have panicked Prince, and me as well, for that matter.

If you imagine a large square of plain knitting done by a giant using small fence posts for needles and approximately quarter-inch steel bars for the wool, you will have a good mental image of a chain harrow. Now add large spikes to the underside, and thread a pole along one end of it. The

*The evacuees, 10 children with their teacher on the left
and her mother on the right.*

horse was attached to the pole by means of a whippletree, which was made out of wood, with rings on each end, onto which were hooked the chains from the horse's collar.

A chain harrow was the farmer's equivalent of the gardener's fine-tine rake, and was very useful for raking over grassland. As you can imagine, when turning at the headland you had to swing round in a wide arc. If you turned sharply, which was what Prince wanted to do; the pole would dig itself into the ground and stand up on end, and over would go the harrow. A nervous horse, feeling that happening behind it, was likely to panic and perhaps put a leg over one of the chains – further panic. You could end up in a nasty tangle and a horse would damage a hoof if it trod on one of the spikes.

It was a battle of wits every time we had to turn. Prince had to be made to swing round in a wide arc and keep moving forwards. He was convinced I had got it all wrong and I nearly ended up a nervous wreck!

"You look hot," said Frank, when I returned from that exhausting task.

"I am," I replied. "He takes such huge strides and walks so fast that I have just about trotted over the whole of the field. Also he has no idea how to turn with a chain harrow. Thank goodness that field wasn't any bigger!" Luckily Frank didn't keep Prince for very long.

Our smallholding was doing quite well. The hens had been increased to two dozen and my mother was into rabbit breeding in a big way. She arranged it so that there were always two does producing litters simultaneously. The young rabbits were fattened until they were about twelve weeks old, then killed, dressed and sold to our local butcher. For several years my mother provided the butcher with excellent rabbits and they were much in demand.

Of course, as it was wartime there was food rationing for animals too. We were entitled to twenty-eight pounds of cattle cake per month for Rose and some calf food as well. The hens had a ration of layers mash and the rabbits had bran, toppings and oats. It was possible to get all sorts of odd things off the ration, which was just as well because it wasn't easy to get by on what we were allowed. One time we were offered some damaged unspecified meal. It had been in a fire, due to a raid, and it was going very cheaply. We were told nothing about it, just that it was safe for animals. Rose thoroughly enjoyed it and suffered no ill effects. Another time we bought two dozen tins of damaged beef stew. It had been dredged up from a cargo ship that had been sunk in the Thames estuary. Unfit for human consumption, it was on the market as dog food. All the tins were damaged, some were blown and I made an awful mistake opening one of them! At least I had the sense to take it outside. I put it on the ground, and crouching down I hit the tin opener into the tin with a hammer. A jet of gravy shot into the air, missing my nose by inches on the way up, and landing on my head when it came down. I had to wash my hair immediately. It brought back happy memories of that goose egg ten years earlier, though fortunately there wasn't the pungent smell of sulphurated hydrogen!

A delicacy we found for the hens was known as Tottenham pudding, and came in a huge tin. The hens thought it was delicious. It was made from all the waste food that could be collected in London, boiled for a long time and then tinned. It was revolting stuff, like very thick grey mud, and contained string, razor blades and all sorts of strange bits and pieces. We didn't try it again.

I had decided that we ought to be able to produce more from our five acres and became an avid reader of the *Farmer and Stockbreeder*. I was sure that sound advice could be gleaned from its pages. Two other magazines, named *Poultry World* and *Fur and Feather*, had been my mother's reading matter for many years, as we had kept hens, on and off, since 1932. She now added *The Smallholder* to the list and we had no excuse for not knowing what to do. Our first plan was to extend the vegetable garden by ploughing up a strip of the field. Jim did that for us one Saturday and I borrowed Kitty and the cultivator to break up the ground. It took a considerable amount of work to get a good tilth as this was an old field, which had probably never been ploughed. Now we could grow turnips, thousand-headed kale, marrow-stem kale for Rose, the calves and the sheep, and Jerusalem artichokes for the rabbits. They had the leaves and we had the roots. It was a system that worked extremely well. By the time the artichokes were ready for harvesting in November, Mum had fed most of the leaves to the rabbits. It was done carefully so that enough leaves were left for the plants to produce a reasonable crop of artichokes. The sheep did well on the thousand-headed kale. Rose went dotty over the marrow-stem variety and they all of them liked turnips. Only one or two could be fed to Rose, because one of the most appalling flavours is milk tainted by turnips.

Onion-flavoured milk is to be avoided too!

Early in the year we rented a small field of about one and a half acres just across the lane from us. It belonged to The Boot public house at the top of the lane. I put Rose in there and closed half of our big field for hay

Hens on the dung heap.

by putting a temporary barbed wire fence across it. From the *Farmer and Stockbreeder* I learned about silage making and decided this would make good winter feed for Rose. We bought a wire mesh silo and the sisalkraft paper with which to line it, and also gallons of molasses, which came with a strict warning that it was an offence to use it for cooking purposes. I think you could be fined if you were caught. It was poured into dustbins we had bought, and the smell was delicious.

The next job was to find some suitable grass. It had to be cut when it was young and juicy, and no one wanted to sell us grass for silage. So I decided that we wouldn't make hay from our field, but use it for silage instead. We could always buy more hay. The grass was cut on the first Saturday in June and produced a reasonable crop. I raked it into rows with the hayrake but we did not use the sweeps – we went along each row, picking it up with pitchforks and tossing it into the cart. It was not as easy to deal with as hay because it was wet, and Frank couldn't believe we would get anything worthwhile for Rose to eat. He helped us willingly but he thought we were quite daft!

Making the silage was not all that difficult, but each layer of grass had to be trodden down well before being sprayed with diluted molasses.

As it was a Saturday, my father helped us and did some energetic treading. Keeping the air out was the trick, hence the treading, and if we had got it right the sugar in the molasses would preserve the grass. If we got it wrong, we would end up with hot mouldy grass with a very nasty smell. We finished making the silage in one day, spreading sisalkraft paper over the top to protect it; put baulks of timber on top to prevent the wind from blowing the paper off; and congratulated ourselves on a good day's work. The silage came about halfway up the silo, so we needed to look for more grass.

As luck would have it, Frank was telling a friend of his about our experimenting with silage, and learnt that there was a field which the owner wanted to have cut, because he wanted to put a few horses in it. It was about three acres of old meadow grass, certainly better than nothing. Frank arranged to cut it the following Friday, and we borrowed a lorry and a horse and cart in which to bring it home. We couldn't quite finish packing it into the silo that night and had to leave some for the following morning. By then it had wilted considerably but we piled it in, trod it down and hoped for the best. Now our silo was up to the top. Again we carefully covered it with the sisalkraft paper and weighted it all down. It would compress as the months went by but we were sure plenty of excellent winter feed would be ready for Rose.

In 1941 I had missed the potato planting: it had all been done by the time I joined the workforce. I wasn't so lucky in 1942! It was a tiring job, though nothing like as awful as potato picking. The plough which was used for opening up the rows was called a ridging plough. It turned the furrow both ways, leaving a channel into which the potatoes were planted. First of all, good farmyard manure had to be put in the bottom of the channels and then the potatoes were dropped on top of it, about eighteen inches apart. While we were planting the potatoes the plough was following behind, splitting the ridges and covering the potatoes with earth. On that particular day it was raining, and by the time we had finished it I felt as though I had half the field on my boots. They weighed a ton!

The countryside is always full of surprises and I received a nasty one very early one morning just as it was getting light. In the warmer weather I always slept with both of the windows wide open, no blackout and the curtains pulled back a bit. I awoke suddenly. Something had made a faint noise, but what? I turned my head and there, on my pillow, about six inches from my nose, was a very small bat. This was my second encounter. It looked about as surprised as I felt and sat there licking its lips. I tried to remember if bats scratched or bit, but it was far too early in the morning for clear thinking. I picked up my jumper from the chair by my bed, with the intention of covering the bat, so I could carry it to the window. It must have read my thoughts, for it crawled off my pillow and disappeared down the back of my bed. I heard it as it crawled along under the bed, making a nasty scratching, slithery noise on the polished floor. I waited, wondering what to do. It came out at the end of the bed and made for my shoes. After an awful struggle it climbed onto one and took off. I hastily lay down in bed, the sheet ready to pull over my head. Bats, I had read, never hit anything, but I wasn't taking any chances as my intruder seemed a bit groggy and I slept in the nude! It whooshed round the room, hit the wardrobe and landed on the floor. Definitely not up to the usual standard of bat flying. This time it took off from the floor and missed my nose by an inch. I lay down again.

Both windows were open, but it kept to the middle of the room, fluttered along close to the ceiling, did an amazing nosedive and landed on the dressing table. By now I was getting bothered: supposing it was still doing this when it was time to get up? The bat took off from the dressing table and landed on the foot of my bed. I waggled a toe under it and it took off again, nearly went through the window, turned, came across the bed and landed by my shoe cupboard. I decided the only thing to do was to shout for John, whose bedroom was above mine. Mum was the other end of the house and Pa was in London. I sat up and called. No reply. I called again as the bat took off and did some very bad flying, which took it straight into

The garden, Cottage on the left next to the big barn.

the empty grate. This was definitely a sick bat with its radar out of action. John had finally heard my frantic yells and he stuck his head round the door, nearly receiving a bat in the face.

"Hell's bells," he said, ducking and shutting the door. He wasn't any help at all and remained outside while the bat flew round the room again.

"Where is it now?" he called, from the safety of the landing.

"On top of the wardrobe, looking baffled and unhappy," I replied.

"Grab your clothes and come out now," he suggested, opening the door to take a look at the bat. It chose that moment to try another circuit, missed both open windows, and nearly collided with me.

"I shall not be able to get up," I said, looking at John and taking my eyes off the bat.

"No," he said, looking unconcernedly at me. That was the moment we lost the bat.

"It's gone," said John with relief and returned to his room. I waited five minutes and then grabbed my clothes and fled to the bathroom. After breakfast I hunted high and low but found no bat. I was going to poke behind the wardrobe with a long cane, but changed my mind and decided to ask Phillips to help me. Luckily he always arrived at 8.30, half an hour before I went to the farm, so the minute he turned up we went bat hunting. We found it, hanging on for dear life to a little ledge at the back of the wardrobe. Phillips removed his gardening apron and covered the bat with it. He took it to the window, hooked it onto the creeper outside, and shut the window. At long last, exit one bat!

Chapter Three

One morning I arrived at the farm to find that Frank had bought some little pigs. They were about three months old. He used to do a bit of dealing from time to time and the pigs would be with us until a buyer was found. They had been put in the lean-to shed built onto the back of the barn, and from there they could get out into a small orchard. My job would be to clean the shed out each morning and give the pigs a feed. I very quickly discovered that little pigs have a warped sense of humour! The first morning Frank showed me what to do, and how to prevent the little perishers from getting into the barn. They had deep straw in the shed, which had to be tidied each day and the dirtiest parts removed, before new straw was put down. Then they had their breakfast.

Getting the bale of straw in through the door from the barn without letting the pigs out was not easy. Also I discovered that little pigs squeal "MURDER!" at the tops of their voices if you so much as touch them. So pushing a pig out of the way by giving it a shove with a boot was not to be recommended. The easiest way, I soon discovered, was to put the bale on the floor, open the door a little bit, and quickly roll the bale in. The next job was to open the bale by hitting the wire with a small axe. The wire snapped, the bale sprang open like a concertina, and eighteen little pigs squealed with delight! They thought the whole operation was for their enjoyment and began rooting around under the bale, tossing it about, grunting and squealing with pleasure. It was at this point that I made my first mistake. Having put the axe and the wire in a safe place I seized the pitchfork and stabbed it into the straw and into the back of a pig, which was underneath. The ensuing yell of "Murder!!" was so intense that Frank came running to find out which one I had damaged. I reassured him, and as no pig was bleeding, he retired. The pigs were watching me closely, as though expecting something to happen, and when I scattered the straw about, they rushed madly to and fro. One little nuisance caught me behind my knees and I fell forwards. The little pigs squealed with glee and dashed around even more. The same thing happened a few minutes later and I swear it was on purpose. There was one pig which watched me more than

Phillips, 1937.

the others did and I think he was the ringleader. When he squealed they all squealed.

The next job was breakfast. They were fed on pigswill, made by boiling anything and everything, but in this case mostly root crops plus some greens, in a copper. When it was well cooked it was mixed with some middlings and bran, to dry it off a bit, and the smell was excellent: very much like the hot mash we fed to our hens each morning. Getting the food to the little pigs was even more difficult than dealing with the bale of straw. They could smell the excellent concoction and were very excited. I had two huge buckets filled to the top, which somehow had to be manoeuvred through the door, at the same time keeping the little horrors in. It was possible, but it meant going in sideways and pushing protesting pigs out of the way with a bucket. Shutting the door meant placing a bucket on the floor and that meant cunning pigs would try and get a quick mouthful. They trod on my feet, they tried to knock me over, they were naughty and exasperating. When I reached the trough it had been filled with straw, on purpose, of course! It didn't matter what I did: some pigs always managed to be under the food as I poured it into the trough.

After three days of battling with the little porkers I thought I'd try shutting them in the orchard while I cleaned their pen and fetched their food. Getting them outside was far harder than it sounds. I walked out, calling to them, and they all rushed after me. Then when I turned to go back they all turned too. On the first occasion they beat me to the door. I tried again. Once more I enticed them all outside, and then I rushed back as fast as I could. I just managed to beat them but the ringleader had his head in the door as I tried to shut it. I pushed him out. "MURDER!" he squealed at the top of his voice and all the little pigs copied him. Frank arrived. I explained what I was doing. He looked out at the pigs, who were now playing tag.

"Leave them in when you have fed them," he said. "There's a man coming to look at them."

I cleaned their pen extra carefully and mixed them a special breakfast. After all, with a bit of luck those little pigs would have a new home by evening, and I wouldn't have to battle with them tomorrow. When I opened the door to let them in I did not move out of their way quickly enough. One caught me behind the knees and down I went. In the afternoon Frank told me the pigs had been sold. I watched them being loaded into the pig float, squealing loudly they left for a new home, and I am glad to say that was the only time I had to deal with little pigs!

It was sheep shearing time and I was allowed home a bit early one afternoon to supervise the shearing of our "flock". The man arrived with an incredible contraption, which turned out to be an ancient hand-driven mechanical clipper. When the contraption had been set up, his mate turned a handle, which operated the clippers. Quite effective, and much quicker than the old scissor-like shears. One sheep was nicked on the chest under a front leg. We treated it with that versatile and useful remedy for many ills, namely Stockholm Tar. The charge for shearing was minimal and he had the six fleeces as well. Years later I kicked myself for having parted with the fleeces.

Three weeks later we had to dip the sheep. This is a regulation dipping against scab, a disease caused by a mite, which has to be carried out after shearing. In those days the local policeman had to be notified and he attended the dipping to make sure it was carried out correctly. As the sheep had to be totally immersed for one minute, the operation took place in Frank's yard, using his huge trough. It took three of us to drive six sheep up our lane, across the road and into Frank's yard. Six sheep could be as much trouble as sixty, and ours always worked in pairs. Two of them rushed into the milking shed just up the lane and were chased out by Mrs Martin; two tried to get through the hedge into the garden behind the pub; and two turned left towards Chipperfield when they reached the road. The policeman, Mr Barker, watching from Frank's yard, was enjoying all this.

Dipping went off without any trouble, except that six sheep in a large yard do take some catching! Then we had to drive them home. Everyone stood out in the road so the sheep had only one way to go: straight across. The experience of being dipped had quietened them down and we had no trouble going back down the lane. We even managed to get them through the drive gates and then we found Rose, inquisitive cow that she was, standing by the orchard gate. She wouldn't move to let the sheep in and they wouldn't walk past her. I dashed off to find something tasty to bribe her with and, finally, the sheep were back in the orchard.

Haymaking time was round again, and we were off on our rounds of the local farms helping to gather it in. George, who was Frank's ploughman, shared the mowing with Jim. This time I found myself driving the hay turner as well as the hayrake. The hay turner had two sets of whirling tines which flicked the swathes over. Haymaking is entirely in the lap of the gods. If the weather is good there are no problems and the hay will be lying out for only two days, which means it is of a far better quality than that which has been drying for a long time. If the weather is fickle you can be messing about, turning the hay, spreading it out, tossing it about, anything to get it dry. Young grass takes longer to dry, and if the weather permits a June cut, it requires a very hot sun to get it dry. In fact I do not remember making any hay in June – I think it was more likely to be July before we were able to start. Later in the season the grass is much tougher and less nutritious, but doesn't take so long to dry. The advantage of early cutting is the fact that there is a good chance of a second crop in August, but it all depends on the weather. If all went according to plan, the haymaking would be over before we began harvesting in August.

One Friday in August we were working frantically to gather in a large field of wheat, because the weather was becoming unsettled, so I offered to help on the Saturday as well. I assumed I would again be helping to load the carts in the field. Frank came up to me as I put my bicycle in the hedge, along with the others.

"You'll have to go up on the rick and help Didi: we are one man short today." Oh, good heavens, up on the rick – I hadn't done any rick building yet.

"What on earth will Didi say?" I asked anxiously.

"Quite a bit, I expect," said Frank.

"But," I protested, "he usually has someone up there that knows all about it." It was no good, I couldn't get out of it. I had to be on the rick.

We were working with a pony-powered elevator and the best way to describe its efficiency is to use the word "spasmodic". The pony was bored – who wouldn't be if confined to walking round in a circle all day – and took frequent rests. The duration of each rest depended on the number of suitable missiles within the reach of the man feeding the elevator, and anyone else who just happened to be around at the time. The farmer's two youngest children were given the task of keeping the pony going. They got equally bored and would disappear from time to time. That's when the missiles came in handy. At the foot of the rick we had a small pile of suitable objects. Old potatoes from the remains of last year's clamp; small stones there would do no damage to the pony, and sticks of various sizes. When the pony stopped an object would be hurled at its rump, which was the part most likely to produce some reaction. Everyone shouted at the same time and banged on anything that would make a noise. The pony would, reluctantly, resume its monotonous plodding.

I went up the ladder to the top of the rick, trod in a gap between two sheaves and ended on my face. Ricks in the process of being built felt very unstable and springy because the sheaves had not compacted. I picked myself up and removed some thistles from my hands. Didi looked at me.

"You've never done any rick building before," he stated accusingly.

"Never," I replied, feeling remarkably inadequate. He walked to the edge of the rick.

"Frank," he called out, "I'm not having this girl…" (He knew my name quite well) "…up here with me."

"Then you'll build it on your own," replied Frank. His tone of voice clearly indicated he wasn't going to argue the case.

Didi grunted and turned to me. "Right," he said firmly. "I want each sheaf passed to me butt end first and I expect it to land beside my right hand like this," and he indicated exactly how close to him it must be placed. "I don't expect to have to turn around to look for it," he added. "I expect to put my hand down and there it is. Got it?" I nodded. "You do know how to use one of those, don't you?" indicating the pitchfork.

That was adding insult to injury and I made no reply. "I don't want to be stabbed by it," he concluded and retired to the far side of the rick.

I staggered to the edge. "Right," I called. "Let's begin." The pony, which had gone fast asleep standing up – and, to my amazement, they really could do so – woke with a start as Frank smacked it smartly on the buttock.

"Come on, you dozy critter."

The pony completed half a circle and stopped. I waited expectantly by the top of the elevator while those on the ground tried encouraging it to begin the day's work. It took quite a while and by the time the first sheaf reached me I was not paying attention and it landed on my head. It had a mass of thistles in it and was very painful! Didi groaned and waited for me to pitch it to him. Slowly I turned it round and slung it, butt end first, in his direction. He impatiently caught it and put it in place.

We were still building up the eaves, which meant that every outside row had to protrude a bit beyond the row beneath so the rick would be narrower at the base than at the eaves. This was to ensure that the rain dripped off the edge of the thatch and on to the ground, and did not run into the rick along the straw.

For a while the pony worked at a steady slow plod and the sheaves arrived with a reasonable time interval between each one. I found that walking about on what felt like a huge pile of pillows did tend to make me less than nimble. Every now and then I would half disappear as a leg slipped down between two sheaves, and to begin with I even managed to fall over or sit down abruptly. This, of course, happened as I was about to pitch to Didi and he would have to wait while I regained my balance.

The pony continued its spasmodic walk...round...and...round... stop... wait for the shower of missiles, then ears back in anticipation of the noise we were going to make as we hit everything available. The rigmarole having been completed, the pony was off again, the sheaves jerkily travelling up the elevator.

The "mock well" as a feature, built in 1937.

Then the children reappeared. One child grabbed the bridle; the other hung on the pony's tail; and it came alive. It just about doubled its speed and I suddenly found myself with an abundance of sheaves. Didi was by now at the far right-hand corner, busy doing the neat three-sheaf turn, two at right angles to one another and the third one on top between. In my haste to clear the backlog of sheaves I somehow managed to sling two at once. Didi grunted and threw one sheaf behind him. I was just beginning to think I would be buried under a mound of sheaves when the pony stopped. The children had disappeared, so it was back to the missiles.

The day continued; during one particularly long pause Didi came across and told me I wasn't doing too badly and he would teach me how to build a rick. I did a whole round, not on the outside, but about halfway in, with Didi passing me the sheaves. They were placed by my right hand as he said they must be. But the thistles in some of the sheaves were big and painful. I really needed gloves. I wasn't sorry to go back to pitching!

A few days later Didi was again helping with rick building on another farm near Bovingdon. He saw me come into the yard.

"Come up here," he called out. "You'll help me build the rick, won't you?"

"Certainly," I replied, but at that moment Frank caught sight of me and beckoned.

"Go and rake over the field – the hayrake's ready," he said.

Didi made an awful fuss and called out to Frank that he particularly wanted me helping him. But Frank, who was genuinely hard of hearing, was totally deaf that morning and Jim worked on the rick with Didi, both men building it to speed things up. I retreated to the field to rake up the stray bits of straw.

Poor Dolly had died during the previous winter so any of the other horses that happened to be unoccupied now pulled the hayrake. On this occasion it was another Kitty, known as young Kitty so as not to be confused with the other one. She was a tall, slightly nervous, high-stepping creature, with a damaged hip from a road accident. She was a bit stiff in her right hind leg, but otherwise perfectly all right. I spoke to her as I approached and she woke up with a start. We eyed one another; I never was entirely happy when working with young Kitty and she obviously knew it! I untied her from the gate post and turned her and the rake round to face into the field, and then I unhitched the reins. She was one of those horses that couldn't wait for you to get into, or onto, whatever she was pulling. Once she knew you had unhitched the reins she was off. You couldn't hop onto a hayrake as with a milk float: you had to climb onto it and I was not the sort who relished doing the equivalent of a circus act to gain the seat. Whatever I did, Kitty refused to stop long enough for me to climb up, so I had to go back to the gate and find someone to hold her.

Raking a cornfield was a boring job in many ways because there wasn't all that much straw lying about, and if it was a small field probably one line of straw down the middle would be necessary. Raking was, however, essential because longs wisps of straw would interfere with the ploughing by getting stuck between the coulter and the share. The binder cut the corn very close to the ground. That left short stubble, which need not be burnt, and by raking off the straw one ensured that the field was ready for muckspreading and ploughing.

Kitty was the sort of horse that jumped at almost any noise. The field was roughly six acres and one line of straw was sufficient, so the rake was not being tipped very often. The first time it happened she broke into a smart trot. Trotting with the rake was not to be encouraged because the straw would get left behind. I calmed her down as best I could but she was now alert and expecting the worst. She would have liked to have done the whole field at a smart trot. I heaved on the reins and forced her to walk. Her ears twitched incessantly. "I don't like this," she semaphored.

"Slow down, Kitty," I replied. "My arms are beginning to ache."

I found that by talking to her before I tipped the rake, she was far less likely to react. Eventually the field was finished and one slightly lathery horse was tied up to the gate post. She nearly always managed to sweat a bit under her collar and saddle, and I wondered if it was the result of the accident.

Kitty had her uses though and she was the horse that took us to Watford market on a number of occasions. She trotted well and could take us quite speedily to Watford. She had a tendency to wander to the right: possibly her stiff leg was responsible, so she had to be driven with a bit of left-hand rein in traffic, just to make sure she kept to her side of the road. I was allowed to drive when we were in the lanes, but Frank drove her into and out of the town. I very much enjoyed our trips to Watford. Our route took us through Chipperfield, Bucks Hill, Bucks Hill Bottom, Chandler's Cross, Croxley Green and all the back roads to the market. It was on one of these trips that I had my one and only sighting of a red squirrel, sitting at the edge of Harracks Wood. It glanced up as we trotted by but never moved and they are usually very shy.

During the spring my mother had put four broody hens on clutches of eggs and raised about thirty-six chicks. The pullets had been put in a large pen as they would become the layers when they were about six months old, and the cockerels were in two moveable chicken arks. We had mainly Light Sussex hens with a few Brown Leghorns and a Light Sussex cockerel running with them. Mum had been able to buy a large quantity of kibbled rice. It looked very old and was remarkably dusty. Cooked in skimmed milk it made a grey rice pudding for the cockerels, which they ate with gusto and thrived on it. At twelve weeks old they were sizeable birds and ready for killing. Some we ate ourselves, but many we sold to the butcher to help with the meat ration, which was very small.

Hens are not the totally bird-brained creatures they appear to be. Some can be quite tame and friendly. We had one hen which was a cross between a Brown Leghorn and a Rhode Island Red. She was known as Auntie, because she was a very good mother. She would not lay her eggs in the nest boxes in the hen house. Every day she got out and laid her eggs behind a large clump of chrysanthemums in the front garden. We never saw her get out of the hen run but we were pretty certain she flew over the six-foot-high wire netting. Her wings were clipped to prevent her flying, but she still laid her eggs behind the chrysanthemums. Someone told us hens could run up netting, but how could she fly down with clipped wings? We never did solve the mystery. Because she was a good mother we kept her for many years, but in the end she stopped laying and had to go. She was one we couldn't eat: she was almost a pet and frequently was found wandering round the house if the front door was left open in the summer.

Front gate, known as the hole in the wall.

I think it was during the summer of 1942 that my father decided he would have some ducks. He had a great fondness for duck eggs and they made delicious cakes. We had four Khaki Campbell ducks and for some inexplicable reason, two drakes. Pa helped to look after them at weekends – in fact I believe he quite enjoyed doing some of the odd jobs around the place. The ducks all did very well. They were placid, friendly, and no trouble at all except that they would lay their eggs anywhere that took their fancy. Sometimes it was days before we found them. We had a suspicion that some of the other animals were eating them. Cosmo had a fondness for eggs and I wouldn't have put it past Rose to eat one. She also had a passion for baked apple skins and would gobble them up, dribbling copiously at the same time. If she was anywhere near the wheelbarrow when it was loaded with refuse for the compost heap, she would not move until she had given it a thorough inspection and removed the titbits she liked best. Marrow skins and onion skins, for a start!

One day a stray female cat walked into the big barn, inspected it carefully and decided to stay. She was black with white paws and a white shirt front. A middle-aged cat, she settled down and within a few days had produced three female kittens. They were beautiful; one black and white, one tortoiseshell and one pure black. I have a passion for cats, which was not shared by my father, and he could see the place becoming overrun. However, when the kittens were about six months old, Muff, as we had called her, drove them away and we never saw them again. Her next litter was three toms. She spoilt them, and still hunted for food for them when they were big enough to catch a mouse or two. Her next family was just two tabby toms. With their arrival the three big toms, Whisky, Blackie and Nervous, suddenly found they had to fend for themselves. We always gave them milk and titbits if they were hungry, but there were plenty of rats, rabbits and mice for them to catch. The three lazy creatures used to sit watching their little brothers eating and if one of them so much as twitched a whisker he would be hit on the head by Muff. Finally, they got the message and set about hunting for themselves. Nervous became semi-wild, hence the name, and would never come near enough to be stroked. Blackie had the most beautiful hazel eyes I have ever seen on a cat, and was my favourite. He was loving and gentle. Whisky was a thief and spent most of the day in the kitchen, sitting on top of the hatchway, which communicated with the dining room. He watched the cooking through half-shut eyes and was ready to steal anything he could. Only one of the tabbies survived. For some reason Neda killed one of them and nearly castrated the other but he survived. He was never a very big cat and was called "Chat" after chat potatoes, which were small, unfit for human consumption and sold for animal feed.

The Smallholder magazine was filling my mind with all sorts of ideas. I was sure we could produce more animal feed from our land. We had to buy hay, mangolds, swedes and some potatoes. These were the chat potatoes, dyed purple to indicate they were unfit for human consumption. I was sure we could grow more of the kales and possibly some swedes for the sheep and Rose. In *The Smallholder* I saw an advertisement for a pony plough. If we had a horse we could do all the ploughing and harrowing that was necessary for the crops we wanted to grow. It did mean buying a horse and the necessary harness.

The first pony we bought cost us eighteen pounds and we kept her for one week. She was elderly and bad tempered. I suspect she had not been treated very well because she was easily startled. I tried to be nice to her but I was not prepared to put up with a horse that bit anything handy when having the girth tightened. Also she was nearly impossible to get between the shafts of the old milk float we had bought. She had another nasty habit of rearing when in the shafts, which I found quite terrifying. We called her Peggy, a female Pegasus because she rushed everywhere. At the end of the week I returned her and got my money back. I had been taken for the sucker I was and it taught me a good lesson. So all my grandiose schemes were put aside until something better in the way of horseflesh turned up.

We had finished the haymaking and harvesting; autumn was here and dung, or muckspreading as it was usually called, was imminent. Muckspreading was done before the ploughing and we did it the old-fashioned way. Piles of manure were dotted about the field and several of us, armed with dung forks, hurled it about to spread it as evenly as possible. Some farmers had to buy extra dung if they had too few cows and horses to provide enough for their own requirements. So dung carting was another of my jobs. For this I mostly had the old plough horse, Dick. He was very placid, lazy, and a bit slow. His big advantage, as far as I was concerned, was that nothing upset him. He knew what he had to do and he always did it. He was a most even-tempered animal and I grew very fond of Dick. His ploughing partner, Captain, was several years younger and a bit bigger. They were a rather ill-matched pair because while Captain wanted to get on with the job, Dick on the other hand, couldn't see why there was any urgency. Dick was the furrow horse and would not be rushed. Captain had the easier task: he was walking on firm land.

My first trip with the dung cart took me to Sarratt to load up. The return journey brought me down the steep hill into Belsize, with a big load. Dick could hold a load well. He only took small steps and settled well back into the breeching straps. But horses can slip: their metal shoes do not grip the road, so a brake is necessary. There were no brakes on any of Frank's carts, only on the four-wheeled wagon, but there was a device which could be put under the nearside wheel. Called a skid, it was a strip of metal, slightly wider than the wheel, and with sides so that when in place it couldn't slip sideways. It was attached to the cart by a chain and when not in use it hung just under the nearside shaft. Unfortunately, by 1942 it was illegal to use skids. They were bad for the road surface.

"Don't let a policeman see you with the skid on," said Frank as I left the yard.

In Sarratt I helped load the manure.

"You wouldn't have done this by yourself?" I was asked when I was about to leave.

"Yes, if I'd had to," I replied. "But," I added, "it would have taken me quite a while. I'm glad you were able to help me!"

I said goodbye and Dick and I headed for home. At the top of the hill I hopped down and put the skid in place. There was nobody about. Dick began a slow, careful descent of the hill. I was leading him: even with skid on I was not going to be up top, just in case something happened. Unfortunately, with one wheel immobilised it was only too obvious from behind that a skid was in use. Also on looking back I noticed there was a telltale mark in the loose chippings by the side of the road. But I did not have the courage to move out a bit – I felt safer near the hedge. If anything went wrong I could pull Dick over and wedge the wheel against the bank. Dick took the hill very slowly and we turned the corner at the bottom, in Belsize, without mishap. All the way down I had an awful feeling that I would meet the local bobby. Only one van and one man on a bicycle passed me and I heaved a big sigh of relief when we were on level ground again and I could remove the skid!

We collected manure from any farms with a surplus and this sometimes meant helping to dig out a stockyard, where cattle had been wintered. The manure was compacted and I found it very hard work digging it out. It would be piled up in a gigantic heap and then collected when ploughing time was round. Muckspreading took place anytime from autumn to January, depending on the weather and when the ploughing was to be done.

On our modest holding we saved all the manure from the calf pen, rabbits and Rose. Every day it was added to the large compost heap at the bottom of the vegetable garden. Hen manure we kept separately, as it had to weather a bit before use.

I was impatient for threshing to begin, but before that we had the potatoes to lift. A back-breaking job at the best of times, it was appalling when the weather was wet. It poured with rain for the two days we were at Street Farm, near Bovingdon. It wasn't particularly cold, but we got so wet and it was such a slow job that we all felt miserable! The ridges were split open using a ridging plough and we followed along with buckets, picking up all the visible potatoes. There was a cart near at hand, into which the buckets were emptied. As soon as half the field had been cleared it was harrowed, to bring any missing potatoes to the surface, and two of us went round picking them up. The potatoes were clamped immediately, having first been sorted into two groups: those fit for storage and those fit only for animal feed. Clamps were the only way for storing potatoes unless you had some space in a barn. The clamps were made as long as necessary and about six feet wide. A pit of a few inches deep was excavated and the potatoes were piled as high as they would go, probably no more than about three feet. Then they were covered with wheat straw, and earthed up to within a foot of the top with about a two-inch thickness of soil. That enabled plenty of ventilation for the heat to escape. Then after a few weeks the free moisture in the clamp would have decreased and the final earthing up, to a thickness of about eight inches, could be done. Little chimneys of straw were left sticking out of the top to allow a certain amount of aeration. At home Phillips was clamping our potatoes in the same way. We had also grown a lot of carrots and those were stored in sand. Again a small pit was dug, but it was circular and the carrots were laid in rows with their tops facing outwards and sand sprinkled liberally around them. Each row started one carrot length in so you finished with a circular pyramid. Plenty of sand had to be built up round the sides and patted in place, to make sure it was frost proof. It was like playing sandcastles. In the spring the remaining carrots began to sprout and before we had emptied the clamp there were always some carrot shoots showing through the sand. It was a good way of storing them.

At last threshing time was here! Once again we began at Bulstrode Farm and this time Percy had both bays of his huge barn packed to the roof: oats one side and wheat the other. We had the full set too: baler, trusser, chaff cutter and elevator. The drum was inside the barn with the engine outside one door and the trusser outside the other.

*Ruby, 1938, died from distemper in 1939. Only strict quarantine
saved Goldie, her puppies and Cosmo.*

This time I was taking no chances and I went well wrapped up, with
twine tied round my trouser legs as an anti-mouse and anti-cavings pre-
caution, as well as a scarf round my head and one round my mouth and
nose. They were well underway when I arrived and a pile of cavings met
my eyes. I grabbed a fork and began moving the useless stuff out of the
way. They had begun with the wheat and had the trusser working.

This was a good straight straw – not too much leaf, and would be ideal
for thatching, so Percy was having it trussed and a rick was being built
outside the barn. As recompense for all the hours of cavings removal I had
done the year before, one of Percy's men asked me if I would like to be on
the trusser instead and he would look after the cavings. It made a marvellous change and I spent the day tossing the trusses to the pitcher, who was
feeding the elevator at the foot of the rick.

On a dead tree sat a huge white owl. It had been roosting in the barn
right at the top, when the tackle arrived. Apparently it had eyed the tur-
moil below with increasing concern. Finally, it could stand it no longer and
flapped its way slowly out of the barn, to settle in the tree. It looked miserable sitting out there blinking in the daylight. When they shut down that
evening it flapped back in again. I presume it had forty winks and then
went hunting for food. The next morning I was there when the day's work
began and was able to witness the owl making its exit from the barn. I felt
sorry for the big bird: we had totally destroyed its peace.

By now T T Boughton had to take on more men to man their stead-
ily increasing fleet of threshing sets. It meant occasionally recruiting some

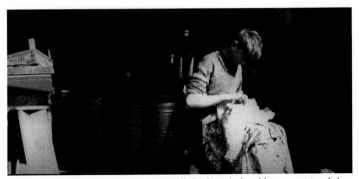

John in big barn plucking a hen. All the bins behind him contained the rations for the rabbits, ducks, hens, sheep, calves and Rose.

drivers who, in normal circumstances, would have been regarded as unsuitable. When John Boughton called one lunchtime at a farm in Chalfont St Giles, to issue instructions for the next day, he found the driver sitting by the back wheel of the engine, drunk, singing God Save the King. He was the same driver who boasted on one occasion of drinking thirteen pints of Benskins best bitter at lunchtime and then cycling back to work. In those days he drove a roller. I wonder what the road looked like that afternoon after he had rolled it!

The threshing drum fascinated me and I asked if I could go up top and do some feeding, but both Frank and Didi flatly refused to let me. Didi told me there was no guard of any sort and if I fell in I would be very seriously hurt, if not killed. Some thirty years later, at a traction engine rally, I was invited up top to take a look at a drum that was idle. I appreciated, for the first time, why I hadn't been allowed to do any feeding.

I still cannot keep away from threshing drums and at a rally in 1978 in Little Missenden I was watching, with my elder son Mike, a drum at work. I was listening, as though in a dream, to the drone, which is music to my ears, when I felt a tap on my shoulder. I turned round.

"A mouse has just gone up your trouser leg," said a man, with just the slight hint of a gleam in his eyes. A likely tale, I thought, though we had seen a few mice dropping to the ground under a nearby trailer full of sheaves.

"I haven't felt anything," I said, smiling, to show that I wasn't about to scream, panic and remove my jeans there and then.

"Well," he replied, "there was one around your feet a minute ago and it has disappeared."

This could be awkward, I thought. I could not undress here and the ladies' loos were a field and a half away. The crowd watching the threshing promptly became far more interested in a woman with a mouse up her jeans. Everyone was smiling expectantly. It was a huge joke to them. At that moment I felt a touch of fur behind my left knee. Oh, blast, there was a mouse and it had been climbing up my jeans, not me, which is why I hadn't felt it. Now it turned round and crawled up my leg. I could feel its tiny paws gripping my knee as it moved round to the front and started climbing up my thigh… Luckily my jeans were a good fit. It would get stuck.

"You are quite right," I said to the man, who was looking all expectant. "There is a mouse and it's here," and I cupped my hand round it.

"Go on. Pinch it," he said. But I couldn't.

"You do it," I replied. He obliged by pinching the mouse hard, but he picked the wrong end and the other end bit me.

"It has bitten me," I announced.

"Nonsense," he said. "Mice don't bite."

"Oh yes they do!" and I stamped my foot hard several times and finally managed to dislodge a half-dead tiny mouse.

"Go on," I said to the man. "You'll have to finish it off." He did so by treading on it.

A friend who was with us asked me when I last had an anti-tetanus injection. I couldn't remember; it was so long ago. He advised me to go within the next two hours and have another. I looked at Mike.

"It will mean High Wycombe Hospital," I said. By now the bite was stinging like hell and blood had oozed through my jeans.

"We'll go in a few minutes," he said. "You go back to the car and I'll join you shortly."

This was the year of the go-slow and work-to-rule in the hospitals. There was a notice in Casualty warning us that the service might be very slow. I decided I had better ring home. My younger son Chris answered.

"We might be a bit late for supper," I said. "I've been bitten by a mouse and I'm at High Wycombe Hospital for an anti-tetanus injection." There was a pause, then peals of insensitive laughter.

"I don't believe it – Dad, Dad! Listen to this – Mother's been bitten by a mouse!" More shrieks of laughter.

"Right, you miserable lot," I said. "I'll see you later."

I approached the nurse at the desk. The casualty ahead of me had disappeared.

"I've been bitten by a mouse," I said.

"You've WHAT?"

"Been bitten by a mouse."

"Are you sure?" she asked.

"Positive," I replied. "It got up my jeans at a traction engine rally…" I stopped.

The nurse was trying to hide her laughter. The young doctor beside the nurse had turned round. His back was towards me and his shoulders were shaking.

"I want an anti-tetanus injection, please," I said firmly and was asked to wait a few moments.

Presently I was shown into a cubicle and in came a male nurse.

"Now where's this mouse bite?" he asked, friendly enough but with the suggestion that I might have imagined it all. I rolled up the leg of my jeans and showed him.

"You have been bitten," he said. "Well, well…a mouse, yes, I can see where the teeth have punctured the skin." I could imagine him saying to the rest of the staff, "That woman claiming to have been bitten by a mouse was right after all!"

When I got home I received no sympathy.

"You of all people… Bitten by a mouse, and you keep telling us about the rats and mice at the bottom of corn ricks and how you all had binder twine round your trousers. YOU forgot something as simple as that…at a rally?" They dined out on it for weeks.

One of the farms we visited during the winter of 1942 had a huge stack of oats to be threshed. It was known to be full of rats at the bottom

The stray cat, Muff, takes her kittens back into the barn.

and several of the men reckoned there would be a bit of sport to be had. The rat wire was put round the rick, ready to catch the wretched rodents when they finally made a run for it. The bottom of a rick was always made with the poorest sheaves whenever possible, because they were always wasted. The rats had bitten through the twine and the sheaves were dusty and dirty. The rat wire was required by law, as the contractor, driver and farmer were all legally responsible. In fact John Boughton spent V E Day in court, answering a summons because the wire had not been put round a rick.

As we neared the bottom, two of the men put their terriers in to catch the rats, which would soon come shooting out. The dogs eyed one another and waited. They both dived for the first rat to appear and I thought a fight would break out. One of the terriers went to the back of the rick and busied himself there. Some of the men armed themselves with sticks and joined in the fun.

Having seen two rats killed I returned to the cavings. Much as I hated rats I did dislike seeing the creatures being cornered. The dogs despatched them quickly. One was bitten on the lip – a nasty bite – and was removed from the fray. Some rats escaped in all the excitement. I can't remember how many rats were killed but I expect it was several dozen. After a threshing session at Bulstrode Farm we always had a few rats in our barn. The ricks having gone, they were on the lookout for a new home. The black-and-white cat, Muff, soon put paid to them.

Tree felling was another activity going on in our area and I loved watching the engines when they were logging. The felled trees had to be pulled out of the wood to the nearest bit of suitable ground, where they could be loaded onto trailers, to be taken to the sawmills. To see those massive engines pulling huge trees along, or, if the ground was muddy, winching them in stages to the loading point, was a sight I shall never forget. Always there was the superb beat of a single-cylinder engine working hard, exerting every ounce of its strength and getting the very maximum energy out of the expansive properties of steam.

Besides taking timber to the sawmills, Boughtons were ordered by the Government to deliver timber to a firm in Penn Street. They were frantically turning out rifle butts as quickly as they could. Just about all the British Expeditionary Force's equipment had been left behind at Dunkirk and there was a massive drive to re-equip. Boughtons were ordered to make three journeys a day from Latimer, where the timber was being felled, to Penn Street. They were not at all sure how they could fit those

The broody hens in coops with their chickens.

journeys in, along with their contracts with local firms. Naturally the last thing they wanted to do was to upset their regular customers. They were stretched to the limit and needed more road haulage vehicles.

Then John Boughton's father remembered seeing a Tasker steam tractor lying derelict near Honiton in Devon, so they bought it for twenty pounds – about two hundred and eighty in present-day money. In a few weeks it had been rebuilt in their Amersham works and was ready to join their fleet.

By using an old Fowler general-purpose engine to load the trailers while the little Tasker was dashing across to Penn Street with a full one, they were able to meet their obligation of three journeys a day. This meant they could use their diesel lorries, of which they had a few, for the local regular customers, so everyone was happy.

An interesting point to that story is that the combination of Fowler and Tasker was just as quick and efficient as using a diesel lorry. Incidentally, when the diesel engine was fitted to lorries in the early 1930s the fuel cost one and a half old pence a gallon and carried no tax. At ten miles to the gallon the cost of a return trip to London was about two shillings – ten new pence!

Chapter Four

The great day arrived. It was time to cut into the silage! We had an old hay knife, found in the barn when we moved in. The local blacksmith had made a new handle for it and sharpened the blade. Carefully we undid the wire frame and folded back a section, then removed the baulks of timber and slabs of cement from the top, and removed a bit of sisalkraft paper. The sight that met our eyes was not encouraging. The top of the silage was very mouldy and the smell was not appetising. Phillips began to cut down into the heap as though it was a big cake. He made a second cut and I removed the paper on the side. Together we pulled out a wedge of dark-brown rich-smelling silage. It was only mouldy on the very top and a bit halfway down where the two different lots of grass met. It had worked! There wouldn't be too much waste, but we would have to remove the middle strip of mould, before feeding it to Rose.

Our excitement grew. What would she think of it?! I tied Rose up in the open barn, where I usually milked her, and then we put a helping of silage into the manger. She sniffed it, took a big mouthful and chewed it carefully, dribbling appreciatively. She swallowed, licked her lips and quickly grabbed another mouthful. The silage was a success.

Our one concern was how to protect it, now the silo had been opened. It proved to be difficult. We had some spare sisalkraft paper and this we used to cover over the cut part, before we put the wire frame back again. It wasn't ideal but it was the only way we could do it. The silage lasted many weeks and Rose thrived on it. Definitely worth trying again.

During the winter the sheep got out, twice. On the first occasion they decided to visit Percy's mangold clamp. Getting them back was a test of endurance. The sheep were not keen to leave the clamp and Percy's dog was under the impression we were sheep stealers. In fact the dog was such a nuisance, that in desperation, I had to go back to the farmhouse and ask if anyone could call him in. In an exhausted state we finally reached the orchard, having galloped over just about all the ploughed fields adjacent to our bit of land. Then two days later they got into our vegetable garden. Mum found them eating the curly kale. She managed to shoo them back through the hole they had made, but was not pleased with the way each sheep snatched another mouthful before returning to the orchard. Mum blocked the hole with a hurdle and the next day the hedge was repaired by the local odd-job man.

While the work was being done the sheep were the far side of the orchard, lying down with their backs to it all. The minute the job had been completed, and the old chap had walked out of the orchard gate, those sheep were up on their feet as one and had rushed over to examine every yard of the hedge. And people think they have no brains!

We were beginning to wonder if it was worthwhile keeping them any longer. They, assisted by Rose, had done the job they were originally bought for, and the orchard grass was in very much better condition. It was a very old orchard. The trees were huge and gnarled. They still produced plenty of apples but the best were right at the top and no one had a ladder long enough to reach them. The apples we could identify were Blenheims, Coxes and Russets. No one knew what the others were and no one could identify a very old, small plum tree which produced the most glorious fruit towards the end of August.

The orchard grass had been extremely coarse and tufty but sheep, a cow, and the use of a chain harrow, had improved it considerably. So the question remained: what were we to do with the sheep? They hadn't been too difficult to look after, but I had discovered there are several ailments they can get.

If you don't watch them carefully, the blowfly will attack during the summer. Frank told me that if I examined my sheep every day, it should never happen. The blowfly, a large green "bluebottle" type fly, lays its eggs on the dirty fleece round the tail of a sheep. I had cut away some of the dirty fleece, but to no avail. I thought I had been examining my sheep carefully enough, but I hadn't, and so one was attacked. The eggs of the blowfly hatch into horrible white maggots which feed on the flesh of the sheep.

When I got back from work one evening, I noticed one sheep standing under a tree, away from the others. She looked very miserable. On examination I saw the maggots – dozens of them. It was a horrible sight: they had been eating that poor sheep on the top of her tail, where it joins the body. She was in a nasty mess. I went back to ask Frank what to do.

"You naughty girl," he said. "I warned you about the blowfly. Did you dip those sheep again as I told you?" I assured him that we had done another dipping in July, using Coopers Liquid 80 sheep dip. What had impressed us most was the dip's ability to remove a nasty wart Phillips had on his hand! The dipping itself had been memorable because we used a very large tin bath, which we placed by the drain in the middle of our yard. The sheep had been shut in the yard and they stood watching as the bath was filled with dip. They were not really keen on being dunked in a bath of water and it suddenly dawned on them that something nasty was about to happen. They tried to make their getaway. There was a small arbour in one corner of the yard, with a gate which led to the field and one of the chicken runs. The sheep made for it and tried their hardest to force the gate. Fortunately for us it held and Phillips grabbed a hurdle and trapped the six sheep in the arbour. It made them much easier to catch.

Each sheep was dragged in turn to the bath, turned over and plunged into the dip. It was just like washing an animated sheepskin rug. We rubbed them all over with our hands to make sure the dip really penetrated the fleece, and topped the bath up from time to time. Only their faces remained above water, unlike the scab dip, where you have to immerse them completely. Hauling a struggling wet and protesting sheep out of a

Old Kitty (she of night cart fame) scuffling the top half of the field.

tin bath is not easy and by the time we had finished we looked as though we had been dipped too! That had been done at the end of July, and here I was with a flyblown sheep.

Jim came back with me to look at the unhappy animal. He brought his hand shears with him. I held the sheep while he cut away all the fleece where the maggots were and picked them all out. Then he washed the damaged flesh with water and on went that cure-all, Stockholm Tar. The sheep was much happier now that she was no longer being eaten alive, and I gave her some food before returning her to the orchard. Her companions came running, bleating, to greet her. They had to examine her carefully and each one sniffed the Stockholm Tar.

Another problem can be foot rot, from wet pastures, and one sheep managed to get that, though why it should in our relatively dry orchard I couldn't make out. Grazing kneeling down is usually a sign of foot rot. Once more Jim came to the rescue and showed me how to pare their hooves, and again Stockholm Tar was used. It was put in the cleft of the hoof.

I liked the sheep, but we had to be realistic. They were not really necessary, and after a further discussion, we decided to sell them and buy more calves for rearing. We said goodbye to our woolly friends with mixed feelings. Cosmo would be sorry to see them go: whenever the opportunity arose he chased them, even though he knew it meant a spank from whoever saw him. He had no hope of catching them because he was old and suffered from rheumatism, but the temptation was too great – he couldn't resist trying. Frank bought them from us and I think they were sold back to their original owner.

Down the road towards Chipperfield village was Frenches Farm, where there was a small herd of cows. They were a mixed bunch of Ayrshires, shorthorns and a Jersey or two, to add cream to the milk. I had to help there for two days, when the farmhand was ill. I was to do the milk round, help with the afternoon milking and the sterilising of the dairy equipment, and also any other jobs that were necessary.

Rose had to be milked earlier than usual and she was not at all pleased. Mum made some sandwiches for me to eat while I did the round – there wasn't time for any breakfast. I rushed down the road to the farm and was just in time to help load the float with the milk crates and some eggs. The book for the milk round was handed to me. It contained the names only – no addresses – and the amount of milk to leave, in case there was no one at home. However, I had to knock on every door, to make sure. I was a bit worried about the lack of addresses so Miss Hawes, whose farm it was, gave some indication of where the people lived. I was told not to worry because Brownie, the horse, knew the round.

Brownie was about sixteen years old, and totally set in his ways. I hopped onto the float, made all the necessary noises to get him moving, flapped the reins on his back, spoke sharply to him and did everything I could; but he remained rooted to the spot. I climbed off the float and approached the head end. Brownie turned and looked at me. He studied me carefully for a moment, as though seeing me for the first time, and then appeared to fall asleep. I caught hold of the bridle to lead him onto the road. He still wouldn't move. Miss Hawes came out of the dairy and spoke to the horse. He woke up and she led him out of the yard. I hopped back onto the float, grabbed the reins as Miss Hawes let go of the bridle, and we were off. He wouldn't trot; he could only walk, and I had a feeling this was going to be the slowest milk round ever. It was.

When we reached the farm again Miss Hawes was out in the road looking for us.

"Whatever took you so long?" she asked anxiously. "I thought there must have been an accident and I was coming to look for you."

"Were we that long?" I asked, knowing full well we had been away ages. I decided I had better tell her the saga of the milk round because she was bound to hear some of it from her customers.

Brownie would not trot at all. Nothing I did, or said, made the slightest difference to him. I treated myself to a stick from the hedge and walloped him on the rump. He lashed out with a back foot. Better not try that again, I thought, or I shall end up with a bad-tempered horse. So we walked for the whole round, and progress was very slow. As for stopping outside the right house, I soon discovered he stopped where it suited him. Sometimes it was between two houses, which meant a call on both, just in case. I think some of the people I called on thought I was touting for customers. I kept explaining I was new to the round, so they wanted to know why I had no addresses! One house was missed, on the way up the lane, because Brownie didn't stop. Luckily the occupant was standing outside the gate when we came back. She was not very pleased.

"You're new to this round. What's happened?" she asked.

Several people wanted to pay for their milk and I was hopeless at mental arithmetic. When there were eggs to be added to the total, I cringed. At one large house I was told off by the cook, because she wanted to pay for last week's milk as well.

"I can't stand here all day while you add up a simple sum. Where did you go to school?" Unthinking, I told her.

"Oh, one of those posh girls' schools. Well, they didn't teach you much, did they?" I agreed and beat a hasty retreat.

"Come back," she called. "You've left some eggs here." I rushed back and collected them.

"Thanks," I called as I returned to the float.

There were indecipherable notes left out; there was money, which I had to note down; some expected change to be left with the milk; and I couldn't understand the method of accounting being used, so I expect I left the wrong change. It was one long nightmare, and still Brownie would not trot.

Luckily nightmares finally come to an end and eventually the milk round was completed. The comments had been many and varied. Some people had missed the local bus because they had been waiting for me.

"Didn't want the milk left out all day," was one acid comment. I had not done very well.

When we reached the end of the lane and turned onto the road to head for home, guess what? Brownie actually trotted! And that was when I spotted Miss Hawes in the road, looking for us.

Ewes with their lambs penned on the lawn.

I helped to sterilise the returned bottles and all the equipment that had been used, which included the churns, the strainer (for the removal of foreign particles), the cooler (for reducing the temperature of the milk to about fifty-five degrees) and the milking buckets. Everything was scrubbed with a solution of hypochlorite, using special bottle brushes and bucket brushes, and then thoroughly rinsed. All the clean equipment was stowed away in a special zinc-lined cupboard, which also had to be scrubbed out every day. Then the dairy floor was hosed down, and that job was finished.

Cows do not like being milked by strangers. They are creatures of habit and prefer to be milked by the same person at the same time every day. Mrs Martin taught me to milk before Rose arrived. She looked after about a dozen cows for her brother-in-law, whose land was adjacent to ours and Percy's. They were all cows with slight problems. Some were recovering from mastitis, which is inflammation of the udder. Some would not adapt to the new milking machines, which were being installed on some of the bigger farms, and some were dry cows with a few weeks to go before calving. Mrs Martin looked at my hands. "Oh dear," she said. "They're very small." Hers, by comparison, were enormous! She looked at all the cows and finally picked the one with the smallest teats, which also happened to be one of the quietest. It took me several days before I could milk that cow properly and strip out the last drops of milk. On the final day, as a prize for having at least succeeded in milking reasonably quickly and efficiently, Mrs Martin gave me a pint of milk. I remember putting it in a pudding basin for the cream to rise to the top. That was when I learnt that Ayrshire milk has 3.8 per cent butterfat, and such small fat globules that it takes the cream ages to rise. Rose, on the other hand, produced milk with about 4.9 per cent butterfat, with large fat globules, and the cream, which was thick and very yellow, rose rapidly.

Milking Miss Hawes' cows proved a rather slow job. She also had looked at my hands.

"Oh dear," she said, echoing Mrs Martin. "They are small." So she picked out six cows with the smallest teats. A good hand milker can do one heavy-yielding cow in about eight to ten minutes, and it became obvious that I was not a good hand milker. The first one, a heavily-milking shorthorn, took about twenty minutes, partly due to the fact that I was having problems with the bucket. At home and at Frank's I used an ordinary-shaped milking bucket, but as Miss Hawes sold her milk to the public, she had to use the regulation bucket with the small opening up at the top but facing sideways. The reason for the shape was excellent: it was impossible for the cow to get her foot in the bucket, and when carrying a full one the chance of something dropping into the milk was very small. It was also nearly impossible for me to get the milk into the bucket. Getting it at the right angle, so that I could squirt the milk into it and not all over the floor, was proving to be something of a problem. Also the hole seemed incredibly small. I did master it eventually, but I would imagine at least a pint of milk was wasted. The cow was not impressed either, and turned her head to see who was milking her. There is something very disconcerting when a cow studies you carefully and then lets out a mournful MOO as if to say, "Get someone else, quickly."

By the time I had done four cows Miss Hawes had finished. My two remaining ones were getting very restless – it was well past milking time as far as they were concerned and they were fed up with waiting. They were also mooing a great deal. Miss Hawes milked one and I the other. My arms ached atrociously – I had never before milked six cows straight off! In fact the most I had ever done was two: one for Jim, if he was going to be late getting back; and Rose.

The next morning Miss Hawes did the milk round and I mucked out the cowshed and swilled the floor, put the feed out ready for the afternoon milking, and closed the doors. Then I did the sterilising of all the milking equipment – a particularly wet job. For it Miss Hawes had special wellington boots, and rubber aprons which reached the floor. They tied at the back and had elastic round the cuffs. Water got everywhere but there was a drain in the middle of the floor. By the end of it all I was remarkably hot. The hypochlorite was not kind to the hands but it certainly got them very clean.

Miss Hawes returned from the milk round smiling, somewhat ruefully, at the complaints from some of her customers. She had made a point of telling each one that I would not be doing the round again! The afternoon milking was a bit more successful, and my muscles didn't feel nearly so sore. Miss Hawes, her cows and I were very glad that next morning her farmhand would be back.

Another job that often came my way was taking horses to the blacksmith in Bovingdon. Dick and old Kitty were no trouble at all. In fact I used to ride Dick – he would amble along probably dreaming of the large feed of oats. A girl with a horse in tow was always a good target for heartless young men! What better than to make the horse shy. With Dick they were always disappointed. The favourite trick of honking the horn just as you are about to overtake had no effect whatever on Dick. He would merely turn a lazy ear in the direction of the sound! However, he was not the blacksmith's favourite horse, because he would fall asleep while being shod and lean on him! Old Kitty was all right too, but Captain didn't like being shod and when his front shoes were being put on he would run his mouth up and down the blacksmith's back as though he was about to nibble him, so I had to hold his head up. But the day I shall never forget was when I had to take young Kitty, the nervous high-stepping mare, to be shod.

She was to go down first thing in the morning, before doing any work. I put her bridle on her and led her out into the yard. She stood looking horribly alert and blinking in the bright winter sunshine. I didn't relish the prospect of walking her for the best part of two miles to the forge – she looked as though she would shy at everything.

I grabbed the short rope dangling from the bit and, taking command of the situation with all the confidence I could muster, which wasn't very much, I led her out onto the road. She was walking with this curious step that a horse employs when it isn't sure what is going to happen. She trod as though the ground felt insecure. Perhaps she realised that no cart or float behind her meant blacksmith. She certainly seemed reluctant as she peered first to the right and then to the left before turning into the road. I had a horrible feeling that this would be a memorable morning and I was absolutely right.

Once on the road and heading for Bovingdon, Kitty strode out. She was a tall horse, as I have already mentioned, and on that day her head was held higher than ever as she peered this way and that, looking for all the things she was sure were just waiting to frighten her. I kept speaking to her, but, apart from banging her chin on the top of my head, she took no notice of me.

The local bus from Bovingdon appeared and I shoved Kitty halfway into a conveniently handy gateway. The next hazard was totally unexpected. A man was busy cutting a high hedge. I could hear the shears at work – so could Kitty. Then suddenly his head appeared over the top of the hedge and the next second Kitty and I were on the other side of the road. She was quivering and looking up at the man, ears semaphoring madly. It was lucky that in those days there wasn't very much traffic about or there could have been a very nasty accident.

I pulled her head down and tried to take control of the situation. We set off again, but she had to walk sideways to be able to keep an eye on the hedge and the man. I finally managed to straighten her up, and snatched on the bit to try and gain her attention, but it came undone. Oh, blast, I thought, as she pushed it out of her mouth with her tongue. She was making me nervous now and I was losing control of her. She held her head higher than ever and I could hardly reach to get the bit back into her reluctant mouth. I had to stand on the grass verge to hook it up. I spoke severely to her, told her what I thought of her and set off once more, full of determination. If only it had been an afternoon appointment, I thought ruefully. A morning's work would have quietened her down a bit.

The next hazard was a paper bag which drifted across the road. Kitty did an impromptu quadrille, then a dog yapped from behind a garden gate and she broke into a smart trot.

"Oh, you stupid animal," I shouted as I trotted beside her. "WHOA." She stopped trotting and we covered the next quarter of a mile in relative peace. A car passed and Kitty took no notice. She really was totally unpredictable. Then I heard a sound that made my heart sink.

Ahead of us and on the left was a long drive, leading to a house that had been taken over by the army. A lorry was wending its way along and I estimated it would reach the road as Kitty and I reached the entrance to the drive. The sensible thing to do was to cross over onto the other grass verge – which at that point was very wide – to be as far away as possible. I had been crossing and recrossing the road to make use of both verges. It seemed much safer than plodding along, or trotting along the road.

Kitty and I had just reached the sanctuary of the grass as the lorry reached the end of the drive. The soldiers whistled and catcalled, honked the horn and banged on the doors and on the tailboard, making a terrific din. Kitty obliged them by swinging round and backing smartly into the ditch, which terrified her, so she leapt out, straight onto my foot. I was wearing good stout farming boots, but it felt as though my toes had been crushed and I let out a yelp of pain, which the army thoroughly enjoyed and served to frighten Kitty all the more, so she pranced around blowing through her nostrils.

One of the soldiers called out laughingly, "Shall we help you?"

"No thanks," I called back. "She's very nervous. You've frightened her enough." They roared with laughter, waved and drove off. Men, I thought; typical, blasted men! My foot hurt, my pride hurt even more and there was still half a mile to go. What, I wondered, lay in store for us round the next corner.

Kitty snorted and looked at me as though she was seeing me for the

Spitfire and Hurricane (mother and daughter, feisty rabbits who always produced litters of 12).

first time. She then put her nose between my shoulder blades and pushed hard. It was so unexpected that I ended on all fours. As luck would have it I did not let go of the rope or she would have been away. She tossed her head high in the air, which at least helped to drag me to my feet, as I struggled up from the grass.

"Oh, you beastly horse," I cried in desperation and pulled her after me across the road. From that side I could see round the bend and – oh, no! I don't believe it – it can't be true! Road works. A cement mixer, a compressor and that awful drill. None of them was working, but knowing my luck the whole lot would have started up by the time I reached them. Kitty had quietened down again and a relatively obedient horse walked beside me as we tackled the last quarter of a mile and the final hazard. As we got nearer I realised the compressor was in fact working. I only hoped no one would begin drilling until we had reached the haven of the blacksmith's shop.

I crossed the road, yet again, to put the maximum distance between myself and the road works. The men finished shovelling sand and cement into the mixer and started it up. At least it didn't make too much noise. The noise of the compressor was much louder by now and Kitty was taking a keen interest in all that was happening. She was waving her nose up and down again – a sure sign of agitation and impending doom. For the second time she banged her chin on the top of my head, and then came to an abrupt stop. Oh, blast! I thought for the second time; she is going to try the one trick she hasn't used: she is going to refuse to pass this lot. I tugged. She remained firmly rooted to the spot. I couldn't think what to do. I wasn't going to get behind these massive hindquarters and push!

Turn her round, something seemed to say. Turn her in a circle, get her moving and she'll walk past. Quickly I turned her in a circle and she walked past. I heaved a sigh of relief: perhaps I was at last learning how to deal with horses. The forge was about a hundred yards ahead. Hooray, I thought. Thank goodness the journey is nearly over.

At that moment a shattering roar broke the peace: the road drill had started. Kitty put her ears flat and took off. It was no good pretending I could stop her – I couldn't. We reached the blacksmith's at a very smart trot and shot straight into his shop with a great clattering of large hooves on the concrete floor.

"Good Lord!" said Jack as we burst in. "I wondered what was arriving."

"Kitty," I replied. "A full set please and may I use your phone?" I chickened out and asked Frank if he would come and collect her!

Frank arrived just as Jack finished shoeing the horse.

"Been a bit frisky, has she?!" he asked. "You want to show her who is master. Don't let her think you are frightened of her. Given half a chance some horses will play up." He lit his pipe, tossed the rope over his arm, and with a "Come on, old girl," headed for home.

The road drill had stopped but the compressor and cement mixer were still working. Kitty never saw them. We didn't cross and recross the road to make use of the grass verges: Kitty just walked head down behind her master. "Wrrr," said Frank, as the bus approached on its return journey. Kitty did as she was told and I didn't even know what it meant. Once she put her nose between Frank's shoulder blades. "ARRRR," he growled and Kitty removed her nose. The same dog yapped and the same man was cutting the top of his long hedge. Kitty saw nothing and heard nothing.

In the yard Frank handed me the rope, which had been draped on his arm the whole way back.

"Give her a drink," he said, "then put her in the stable. Jim will be using her by and by." I took Kitty to the trough, unhooked her bit and she plunged her nose gratefully into the cool water. In the stable I rubbed her down with a leather and removed her bridle. She whiffled her nose up and down the manger to see if she had left any breakfast behind. I looked at the big black mare. She was all sweet reasonableness.

"Oh, you horse," I said as I stroked her silky nose. "You blasted horse."

She looked at me, ears pricked.

"Who...? Me?" she seemed to say. "What have I done?"

Some winter jobs were miserable ones. Anyone who has grown a few Brussels sprouts in their garden knows what it is like, on a winter's morning, to have to pick enough for a meal. It is a hundred times worse to pick them by the bushel! The ones I had to pick were covered in snow. If I was cold before I began, I was numb by the time I finished. I began on my own with a horse and cart for company. Luckily the horse was old Kitty and every now and then I warmed my hands by tucking them between Kitty's front legs and her chest. She didn't seem to mind too much. I was well wrapped up in masses of thick jumpers; a pair of my brother's old grey school trousers; his football socks; and a scarf, tied like a turban, on my head. There had been a bit of a disagreement with my mother when she saw me in my brother's trousers. She still regarded it as unladylike to be wearing trousers with a fly opening. Women's trousers in those days always opened at the side. Normally I wore dungarees but these were not very warm round my legs and John's old trousers would be much better. They were, and having got away with wearing them that day, I stuck to them for the rest of the winter.

Not all the winter jobs were as awful as sprout picking! Spring cleaning the cowshed and whitewashing the walls was one of the essential jobs. Repairing the barn roofs and nailing back the boards, which always seemed to drop off the sides, was another. Miss Hawes' cowshed slipped a section of its roof and I had to be Frank's assistant when he mended it. All loose tiles were removed and several of the adjoining ones as well, so that the broken laths could be repaired. I had to stack the tiles carefully, leaning them against the cowshed wall. Broken ones were piled separately. Frank then set about repairing the laths and while he was doing that I was mixing the mortar, which went under the ridging tiles. When the laths were repaired I had to hand the tiles up to Frank for him to put them back on the roof. I learnt quite a bit about repairing roofs but when our barn roof did the same thing, it slipped along too great an area, and the local builders repaired it.

When the weather was dry, creosoting of hen houses, gates, fences and fence posts had to be done, and of course hedging and ditching was a regular winter job. I had to clear away all the wood that had been cut out and either load it onto the cart, or, if we were burning it there and then,

One of the lambs.

feed the bonfire, which had to be out by dusk because of the blackout. I loved that job: I kept beautifully warm! Then there were hurdles to mend, fences to repair, trees to prune – whatever the time of year there was never a dull moment. One job Phillips did during January 1943 was to strip and repaint the old milk float we had bought. He was sure we would find a suitable horse for our needs, so he prepared the float, in readiness for the great day.

On our smallholding the additional kale we had grown on our extended vegetable patch was proving to be very useful. The ration of one pound of cattle nuts per day for Rose was quite inadequate, and her feed included kale, potatoes, a large helping of silage, plus hay and mangold. Frank told me he could get some crushed oats and I added those to Rose's diet. She did quite well and produced more milk than I expected in the circumstances. Guernseys are not heavy milkers: it is quality not quantity with them and she probably produced 500 gallons a year. Rose dried off six to eight weeks before calving, which gave her a chance to build her strength ready for the next lactation. Frank, fortunately, always had the odd cow or two in milk, and I was able to buy some from him each day, until Rose calved again. By the time Rose was dried off the calves would all have been sold, and I would buy two more a month after she had calved again.

With the first two calves I reared, I taught them to drink from small buckets, which is not difficult but is very messy. Week-old calves are skittish, happy extroverts: give them a bucket of milk and anything can happen. To teach a calf to drink you let it suck your fingers then draw its head down into the bucket. A calf's instinct is to suck with its head up under the cow, not down in a bucket, so it will only go down about halfway. Then up it comes and latches onto the nearest thing; which more often than not were my dungarees. Hunger drives them on to try again and before too many meal times have passed, they have mastered the art. Once the milk has been finished, then the happy game of bucket bashing begins. I reared my calves in pairs and there was always one that finished its milk first and would try to get its head in the other one's bucket. It had to be forcibly removed and pushed away and that is when the bucket bashing would start. An empty bucket pushed round by a calf is an unguided missile and I was always having it rammed into my legs. Calves are surprisingly strong and I received many painful bruises during the first few weeks of bucket feeding. There was one calf I had which repeatedly got the bucket on its head and always ended up in a panic.

Having suffered for some time with bruises and cut fingers from the calves' very sharp teeth, I was delighted, the following year, to see in the *Farmer and Stockbreeder* an advertisement for an excellent calf feeder. It was the answer to all my prayers. It was quite simply a large funnel, which ended in a large rubber teat. There was a rubber ball in the neck of the funnel, which acted as a valve. The calves were fed, one after the other, and it worked perfectly. Also I think it was better for them because they had to suck, not gulp, and they took the milk more slowly.

I was lucky with the calves I bought. They all did very well and when sold probably paid for the food they had eaten. Most of them had come from local farms and I knew they were healthy. Buying them from the market was always risky because there was the possibility of disease. I did try my luck once and bought a beautiful Hereford heifer calf, which fortunately turned out to be perfectly healthy.

It was 1943, and spring was not far away. Rose would calve soon and the calf pen had been cleaned out, disinfected, and filled with straw. She had again been served by the Ayrshire bull the previous August. I wanted a heifer calf because there was something to be said for the Ayrshire–Guernsey cross cows. They were good milkers with a reasonable butterfat count. Though not suitable for breeding purposes many farmers went in for the "first cross" milking cows.

One Saturday I decided to go up to London and use some of my clothing coupons. I came back on the 3.10 local train – Euston to Bletchley, first stop Watford Junction. It was a semi-fast headed by a fairly big engine, but this turned out to be a faster than usual journey. The train left from one of Euston's out-of-the-way platforms, probably number 13. In the rear two coaches were Americans returning to Bovingdon Airfield. I chose one nearer the front and the compartment contained a Chinese gentleman in one far corner and a nun opposite him. She was busy with her rosary and was reading a book. We left punctually and I settled down with my magazine. Presently I heard the sound of a powerful engine, obviously hauling a heavy load, puffing up the long incline towards Chalk Farm.

The engine drew level with our coach. It was very dirty with steam leaking from several places, showing that her maintenance was not very good. She roared as she gathered speed and pulled her load past us, and the fireman could be seen shovelling coal like mad. I was sure that was the last I would see of her. It was a troop train going north. This was the build-up to D-Day. Then I felt a tug as our engine accelerated and before long we pulled ahead. I settled back with my magazine again, but not for long because the train was back, rushing past us, the soldiers leaning out and waving and shouting at the Americans, who were shouting back! So began a spirited race to Watford Junction. Sometimes we were in front, and sometimes the troop train. We tore through Harrow and Wealdstone neck and neck, parting company to pass on either side of the island platform packed with surprised passengers.

Without any difficulty we kept pace with the troop train and then we reached Bushey water troughs. The big engine dropped her water scoop and a sheet of water shot up and plastered the side of the leading coach. The soldiers were frantically trying to pull up the windows. Those leaning out were soaked! Our train had to slow down at this point to negotiate the crossover into Watford junction, and the troop train stormed ahead and was gone. The Chinese gentleman allowed a small smile to tweak his lips but the nun resolutely read her book. I had seen a good-looking blond soldier, but I couldn't reach the window to wave to him!

We arrived at Watford ten minutes early. I hopped down and was making my way up the platform to have a quick word with the engine crew. It had been an excellent run! Out of an office on my left came a tall figure who made his way purposefully towards the engine, where he spoke for a moment or two to the fireman and driver, who were leaning out. I changed direction and went to catch my bus to Chipperfield.

Thirty years later at the Quainton Railway Society I learnt that while the build-up for D-Day was taking place a troop train left Euston at 3.10

on Saturdays, and the semi-fast raced it every time! The troop train was packed so full the guard could not get along the corridor to close the windows. Each time the crew were ticked off but never suspended, due to a shortage of experienced crews. I also learnt that the engine was a Duchess, very powerful and pulling anything up to fifteen coaches and our engine was a Black Five.

Spring turned my mother's thoughts to the next lot of chickens to be hatched. Before she was married she kept a few Barred Plymouth Rock hens, and had always wanted to try them again. There were a rare breed and Mum decided to advertise in *Poultry World* for hatching eggs. Her advertisement was answered and with great excitement we waited for the eggs to arrive. In those days anything and everything went by train and before long the twelve precious eggs were safely delivered.

Auntie was then given the honour of sitting on them. We waited for the three weeks incubation with mounting impatience. When hatching day arrived we kept looking at Auntie in case a chicken peeped through her feathers. She was an excellent mother and had a vicious peck if anyone tried lifting her up to peep underneath. So we had to content ourselves with listening for faint cheeping. Nothing seemed to be happening. The next day, wearing bullet-proof gloves, Mum lifted Auntie off the nest and took stock of the situation. There was one small black chick and eleven infertile eggs! Mum wrote to the supplier to complain, and received a letter saying they couldn't be responsible for the failure of the cockerel and expressed astonishment that the chick was black. But Mum wondered if she had been taken for a ride. The chick grew into a leggy, thin, beaky-looking bird, pure black, and we wondered if it was a cross between a Black Minorca cockerel and a Plymouth Rock hen. It had white legs and could have been a pure-bred Black Minorca, but it died before we found out if it was a pullet or a cockerel or for that matter, what breed, or mixture, it was meant to be. Never again did Mum buy eggs for hatching – we stuck to our own birds. So that was the end of the Barred Plymouth Rocks: we never did have any.

One day, during April, my father phoned to tell us he had heard of a suitable horse. Sue was her name and she had an interesting medical history. She was a four-year-old Welsh cob that had somehow or another dislocated her neck. A young vet, who was a friend of my father's, saw her at market about to be sold for slaughtering. She was a well-set-up cob and the vet was so taken with her that he bought her, with the intention of trying to get her neck back to where it ought to be. He had her in plaster for weeks and did such a good job on her that she was completely restored. Very luckily for us my father happened to hear about Sue and bought her for twenty pounds.

In many ways it turned out to be a good idea. I really did think that a horse was the answer to several of our shortcomings. But first I had to get to know the latest addition to our menagerie. Sue was a gentle animal and because she had been with the vet for a long time she was almost a pet. Luckily she had been broken in very well and was not saddle shy or daft when it come to getting her between the shafts. Also she was not surprised to see dogs, cats, hens, ducks, a cow and, later on, the next two calves.

When we moved to Tenements Farm in 1934, the last thing we imagined was that we would be running a smallholding and that I would be working on a farm. So the small stable, at the arbour end of the open barn, had been made into a room with a view of the field through one window and down to the vegetable garden through another. The third looked out onto the yard. It wasn't long before John and I had taken it over and his

In one end, out the other!

huge "O" gauge Hornby railway was put in there. To my father's annoyance we cut two holes in the wall and ran the train over the coke pile at the end of the barn. I did toy with the idea of converting the room, known as Meadow View, back into a stable, but it would have been an expensive job. Sue was used to being out all the time and it was only in the very worst of winter weather that she slept in at night.

I used Sue for many odd jobs for Frank, but she was not worked hard enough on a regular basis and at times was somewhat frisky. In spite of that Sue and I got on well together. She did not bite, was not ticklish and was very patient. I even tried riding her. I began bareback, but I fell off too often for my liking. Sue had a broad back and I didn't seem able to grip her well enough with my knees to enable me to stay put. So a saddle was the next requirement. I then did a little better and at the weekend Sue and I would venture down the lane towards Kings Langley. She was not inclined to trot when heading away from home, and I used to have a real struggle to get any speed out of her. When we turned round and headed for home she would try to break into a canter, which frightened the life out of me. For a long time a trot was quite fast enough! Sue had a habit of stopping to eat luscious grass, which I found disconcerting. Sometimes, when she felt we were far enough away from home, she would turn round and head back. Many a battle I had trying to convince her that I wanted to go further. To begin with I was the loser, but as my confidence grew, so Sue became more obedient. After some months I did try jumping her over very small jumps, which I set up in the field. I bought a book which told me all about the "forward seat" and banged my nose on her neck as she took off over an eighteen-inch jump! She did quite well, and seemed to enjoy jumping – I was hopeless. Fortunately, when working in harness she was totally obedient and did not suddenly decide it was time to finish and go home.

I think it was at the end of April that Cosmo had to be put to sleep. He was twelve years old and suffering from rheumatism in his hind legs. The vet had warned us that the next attack he got would probably paralyse him, and it did. Mum found him in the lounge trying to get up, but his hind legs would not work. As luck would have it I had just arrived back for lunch and Phillips and I managed to get a sack under Cosmo's hindquarters and lift them up for him. We then walked him out of the house, with his back end on the sack. The front end of him was still all right, but the poor old dog found it a terrible strain, and collapsed just inside the open barn. We made him comfortable and phoned for the vet. Cosmo had never liked Mr Barr and always growled ferociously at him. It was no different this time.

As the vet knelt beside him the old dog lifted his head and fixed him with his dark-brown eyes. A determined, cruel look came into them and a long deep growl rumbled in his throat.

"This will be very quick, old lad," said Mr Barr, as he injected him in the heart. Cosmo never took his eyes off the vet. There was no fear in them and he died growling. Phillips buried him at the bottom of the field and we had lost a wonderful dog.

I think it was just before Rose's calf was due that I suddenly decided we would build a small lean-to cowshed in the field, at the back of the big barn. It would provide shelter for Rose and the calves, and when Rose was grazing in the field it would be much more convenient to milk her out there instead of bringing her into the open barn. Phillips and I worked out the measurements; ordered the bricks, sand and cement from Waterhouse the local builders; and began digging the foundations. We had decided to make the shed big enough for two standings, with small ground-level troughs and a short brick wall as a partition. We knew very little about bricklaying, but just enough to enable us to build two and a half walls with strengthened corners and a sloping corrugated iron roof. The third wall was the back of the barn and the front, which faced south, was to be partly open. We laid a concrete floor and even remembered to fix two tethering rings in the brickwork. We were justly proud of our handiwork, and when everything was dry and it didn't look as though any of it would fall down, we invited Rose to take a look inside.

She examined it carefully from the outside first, sniffing the bricks and then licking one or two. We then encouraged her to walk in and she found the bit of food I had put in one of the mangers. Our measurements had been a bit on the meagre side and Rose had to be careful backing out of the standing, which had the half of the front wall protecting it. But she managed without much trouble. I had not bargained for Sue deciding the shed was her property only, so if the weather was wet Sue found herself in the orchard, so Rose and the calves had a chance to use the shed as a shelter. Also Sue was fond of milk and sometimes she waited outside the shed while I milked Rose, hoping to get a drink when I emerged with the pail. When it snowed during the winter, Rose was in the big barn and Sue had the shed for shelter. That nicely solved the problem of no stable for her.

Chapter Five

Rose gave birth to her calf, attended by Sue, which had not been my intention. I had examined Rose before I went to work and announced to my mother that the calf would not be born before I got home. In fact I predicted it would not be born until the next day. About twenty-four hours before a cow calves, hollows appear either side of the tail and the tail head looks raised. Unfortunately this is a common feature in Guernsey cows. I had looked for other signs. Restlessness is very usual a few hours before calving, but, when I left for work, Rose was lying down contently chewing the cud. Her udder had been distended for a few days and seemed no different and there was no discharge under her tail.

At 3 pm my mother phoned and asked if I could go home and put the calf in the barn, as Sue was far too interested in it and Rose was getting annoyed. Mum had never liked cows and she was not going anywhere near Rose, who was defending her calf from an inquisitive horse.

I dashed back home, to be greeted by two angry mothers! Mum told me in no uncertain terms that as I had known I was going to be out for lunch I should not have left Sue with Rose. Feeling somewhat chastened I removed Sue and put her in the field behind the pub. It was an emergency measure as, strictly speaking, the field was closed for hay, or silage making later in the year. Sue would only be in it for a short time, so I hoped not too much damage would be done. In the event, she spent the time standing by the hedge and neighing loudly. She wanted to know what was happening and I don't think she moved more than a few feet from the gate.

The calf turned out to be another bull. I was disappointed: I had so much hoped for a heifer. It was a big calf and still decidedly wobbly, so I had to carry it. Rose followed me, waving her horns dangerously near my back! I got them both safely in the big barn and encouraged the calf to have its first drink. The first milk is very important for any animal as it is "colostrum", which contains antibodies to protect the new-born from disease. It also sets in a soft curd, which is easy to digest: a very important factor in the wellbeing of calves. The colostrum is at its most concentrated for the first three to four days and the milk cannot be used in the house:

it curdles in tea. There is, however, a beautiful pudding which we used to love. All I did was put a pint of colostrum in a pie dish with a little sugar, sprinkle nutmeg on top and bake it until set. It was very rich and not unlike egg custard. After three days the milk began to change and increase in quantity and then I removed the calf. This caused a day or two of mooing from both of them, and there was also the inevitable struggle to get the calf to feed from the calf feeder. Luckily it didn't take anything like as long as the battle over bucket feeding! By feeding it three times a day there was less mooing from the calf, as it wasn't hungry, so Rose soon forgot it. It was sold at three weeks old and then I set about finding two healthy heifer calves to rear. I was exceptionally lucky and almost at once I found a beautiful heifer, three-quarters Jersey one-quarter shorthorn, which was one week old. She looked pure Jersey and was such a pretty calf that I kept her to be my next milking cow. The other calf was a pure shorthorn.

By now I had read detailed descriptions of the awful things that could happen to calves and I marvelled that there had been no catastrophes with the four heifers the previous year. I always bought the calves at between three and seven days old, just the age when all the diseases were waiting to strike. White scour was a nasty infection which once established on a farm was difficult to get rid of. That was one very good reason for buying the calves from known farms. Then there was joint ill, which was due to bacteria getting in through the navel cord. Again, farms that had the infection could suffer serious losses. Also calves would lick paint, eat sacking or chew binder twine, all of which could cause death. Then there were the diseases which hit the growing calf and I began to wish I hadn't read about all the potential hazards! I must have been very lucky because I never had a sick calf or feeding problems – they were all very healthy. Of course the buildings had not been used for farm animals for many years, so perhaps the possible infections had disappeared.

Up on Tuffs Farm all the spring jobs were now crowding in on us. Winter wheat was due for a good harrowing with tine, or zigzag harrows as they were sometimes called, followed by rolling. The harrowing had to be done carefully so as not to rip up too many plants. Thick crops could be harrowed in both directions. Thin ones were harrowed in the direction of the drills only. There were still many farmers who sowed the seed by broadcasting. It took about a bushel more grain to the acre, but the great advantage was that the seed was well distributed. When drilled in it was in grooves, which made it much easier for wireworms and birds to damage the crop. After harrowing the wheat was rolled with a ring roller, and

Raking up grass for silage making.

that was often my job. I walked miles behind that roller, but it was an easy job, and I had no difficulty turning at the headland, unlike with the chain harrow!

During April spring oats were sown, and had to be harrowed, and that was how I came to be in charge of three horses. Sue was pulling my float, in which I had the harrows and swing trees (same as a whippletree but for two horses), plus lunch for three horses and one human. Hitched on behind were Dick, the old plodder; and Captain, his partner. Captain, as usual, wanted to get a move on and before we had even left the yard, Dick had tried to nip his neck. Out on the road Sue's ears semaphored, "Shall I trot?!" and she lifted her head expectantly. I reined her in a bit as I said, "No, Sue," and she lowered her head and walked sedately along the road. Following behind were the two big horses, Dick's teeth snapping like castanets whenever Captain displeased him.

We reached the field, which was about a mile away, without incident and I managed to convince them all that they were going to stand still while I opened the gate. Some horses always knew best and would move before a gate was fully open, catch a wheel on it and panic. Luckily Sue could be trusted to stand still. Safely in the field I tied Sue to a convenient post, unhitched the other two and tied them to the gate. They waited patiently while I sat up the harrows. It was going to be a boring day for Sue and I removed her from the float, took off her harness and tied her up by her halter, in the shade of a tree. Next I untied Dick and Captain from the gate and backed them up to the harrows and laid out the long reins – made of rope and called plough lines. This was important because very often horses would move as soon as they were both attached to the swing trees. If you had to remove the reins from both saddles before you could control your horse, you could be in trouble. With the reins ready laid out you only had to nip back and gather them up. I always hitched Dick up to his swing tree first: he had no intention of moving until it was absolutely necessary. Captain might think about moving but he had those awful teeth of Dick's to contend with, so he usually just shuffled his feet. Sometimes his shoulder would twitch, as he anticipated a nip.

Frank called in at about 1.30 to see if we were all right. I was having my lunch surrounded by horses. We were all up under the tree and it was funny how the three horses had settled themselves facing me and as close as they could get. We were definitely having lunch together. Sue had her hay – as she wasn't working she did not have any oats. The other two had their oats-and-chaff mixture in nosebags. I used to love watching horses managing their nosebags: they handled them deftly. When they were chasing the last few crumbs they would toss the bag high in the air, so that the last bits could fall into their mouths. Judging by the snorting and blowing that always followed that manoeuvre, the odd bits went up nostrils instead! After lunch we rested a bit and then it was back to work. All so peaceful, with just the songs of the various birds, and somewhere in the far distance, the sound of a tractor working.

Collecting grass for more silage – silo in background.

We were back at the farm by five o'clock. Jim had got home early and put Dick's and Captain's suppers into their mangers and at the same time had solved the mystery of Captain's exceptionally shiny coat. We had wondered if he was eating an egg each day, but so far we hadn't been able to catch him. Normally Captain reached his manger before the food was put in it, and obviously had been able to grab the egg from the corner where it was laid. His secret had been discovered – it was no more eggs for Captain. Mrs Pritchard always looked in Captain's manger first when she collected the eggs during the afternoon.

I had finally succeeded in persuading my father that a small plough would be handy and Frank had a good laugh when he heard what I had bought. I reckoned it would cut down the amount of the time spent digging our extension vegetable garden each year and I am glad to say I was proved right. Phillips and I had hair-raising moments trying to teach Sue how to plough. It took the two of us: one hanging onto the plough, trying to steer it, and the other leading Sue. She couldn't keep straight unless she was led. Several Saturday mornings during April were spent in ploughing. Frank came to have a look.

"Won't be any good," was his comment. "The plough doesn't go deep enough." I didn't argue because I had read that deep ploughing wasn't always necessary if the ground was in good heart, and ours was. It had been well manured with a wonderful mixture of cow and poultry manure plus compost. My idea did work and the crops we produced on that bit of ground were very good.

My next idea was not so good. I decided to plough up the grass across the top of the orchard, adjacent to the drive. It would give us a strip of land about sixty yards long by about twenty yards wide, all to be planted with marrow-stem kale. My small plough most certainly would not make any impression on old grassland, so I had a word with Frank. He thought I had taken leave of my senses and told me I would get very poor results. Marrow-stem kale liked good land, he said. Finally, I persuaded him to send George down to do his best with what was really an impossible task.

George arrived on Saturday morning and took stock of the situation. He was a man of few words, but when he saw what he was expected to plough he became quite voluble! The horses were not going to be very impressed either – there was hardly any room to turn them. George said he would do his best but he also told me that the ground was far too poor to grow marrow-stem kale. After the first furrow had been turned I began to understand what both he and Frank had meant. The roots of the grass seemed to have gone a long way down and the underside of the turf looked matted. Would I ever be able to make a decent seedbed with such awful ground?

"Would it help if you ploughed a bit deeper?!" I asked, anxiously. George set the plough deeper and up came a few flints and an old coin or two! They weren't very valuable, unfortunately, but both seemed to date from James the Second. If my idea did not produce marrow-stem kale I was going to be very unpopular, because the hens had been moved from the orchard to the field; the fence along the top of the orchard had been moved back some thirty yards and I had bought the seed and fertiliser. I was committed to growing marrow-stem kale, come what may.

The horses were not enjoying themselves. They were in danger of falling in the pond at one end of the strip, and when they turned at the other end; they had to lift their heads over the duck's house. Inside the house were five quacking ducks. They were not enjoying the sounds of puffing horses just over their heads!

George did his best and left us with a bit of digging to do at each end to square it up. The soil looked very poor and harrowing it did not produce a particularly good tilth. However, I was confident that the top dressing of sulphate of ammonia, which I planned to apply, would do the trick. Of course I should have spread lots of manure for ploughing in, but I was too impatient and there wasn't much time. It was May and the seeds would have to be in before the end of the month.

There had been a change amongst the poultry, and the flock had been increased to three dozen. Mum had never gone in for the practice of culling all the birds at the end of their first laying season. The best ones were kept on, usually with good results. Naturally they didn't lay as many eggs in their second year but we had several who did quite well. Mum had also bought a Rhode Island Red cockerel in place of the Light Sussex one. Unfortunately the removal of the big hen house into the field presented us with a problem. Rose was a very inquisitive cow, and she was particularly partial to the hot mash which the hens had for breakfast. So when Rose was in the field the hens had to be fed in their house each morning before being let out. Mum hadn't the courage to go into the field on her own because Rose was always waiting to waylay her, so someone had to accompany her. At the weekend it would be my father. Armed with a stick he would precede my mother and go through what can only be described as a bull-fighting routine. Rose, most regrettably, entered into the spirit of the game and pranced around in a most ridiculous manner. She snorted, tossed her head, waggled her horns at Pa and was a much greater nuisance than she was when Phillips or I went in with Mum. Sue would watch from a distance – fortunately at that stage she wasn't sure if it was safe to join in. She had not been with us for very long and had a healthy respect for Rose, who had jabbed her in the ribs with her horns several times. After a few months she got the upper hand and only had to come close, with lowered head and flattened ears, for Rose to get the message and move away.

Frank was not happy. The Ministry of Agriculture had issued an edict about potato acreage and someone had decided that Frank should grow potatoes. He and Jim explained that the ground was unsuitable, but there was no escaping from the order. Frank went ahead and planted an acre of potatoes, in ground that had a high wireworm population. When we harvested them the results were so poor that the entire crop was graded as only suitable for animal feed, so the next year masses of manure was used. The Ministry men had a difficult job I did not doubt, but I am sure there were many times when better results would have been achieved if more notice had been taken of the farmers who, after all, did know what their land could produce.

I think it was during May that we received a visit from the Ministry men. According to them they had confused our land with Mr Martin's and I found them having a good snoop round the back of our barn! They admired the calves and said what a nice place we had, and I noticed that as I escorted them through the barn their eyes were darting everywhere. Perhaps they thought we had something to hide. They certainly asked plenty of questions, but I explained we were a smallholding and didn't come under any of their regulations. Finally, I showed them, on their large map, just where our land was in relation to Mr Martin's and they thanked me and went on their way. A few months later the same thing happened again: two more ministry men had lost their way! There were doing a count of the number of acres down to potatoes and I had quite a job convincing them we were not a farm but a smallholding. They wanted to know what we had in the barn so I took them in to have a look round and after they had gone I fitted a padlock on the barn door.

One morning in May, when I arrived for work, I was greeted by a horribly familiar sight. Frank had bought a number of geese and a gander.

I stood looking at this new gander, remembering only too painfully the nasty bruises I had on my legs from being pecked. Now at least I was wearing trousers and good stout boots, which protected my ankles. I was sure

I would be all right and set about the job of mucking out the stables and cowshed. Coming out of the barn with a truss of hay on my back, I was set upon by the gander. Cowardly bird, he had waited until I was carrying something before attacking. He also turned out to be a cunning bird: he grabbed me just above the top of my boots.

Cosmo's wife Neda had taken over as guard dog and was dangerous because she was a nervous animal. Cosmo never bit anyone. He certainly terrified them sometimes, knocked them down and even bruised one person with his teeth, but he could be trusted never to bite. Neda, without Cosmo, defended the place hysterically and caused us anxious moments. Though we had notices up proclaiming the presence of huge dogs and asking people to ring the bell, occasionally they would come in through the double gates by the barn. I think the notice was not believed by anyone new to the area. Neda nearly bit Pa one night when he arrived home at 1.30 am. Luckily there was a bright moon and Pa saw her as she crept towards him ready to attack.

The marrow-stem kale was successfully sown towards the end of May and I said many prayers so that we might get a reasonable crop. When it finally put in an appearance it was very patchy. We left it until there really couldn't be any more late-germinating seeds, then filled the gaps with cabbages. This unusual move was highly successful and the cabbages grew quite well, helped on with a good dollop of manure under each one. The kale had been top-dressed with sulphate of ammonia and I seem to remember giving it a second dose. I was determined to have as good a crop as possible.

Frank's potatoes were receiving attention too. They had to be weeded using the horse hoe, or harrowed flat and then earthed up again with the potato plough. They had to be watched while growing because of all the blights, fungi, and bugs that could attack them. Colorado beetle was the scare every now and then and all potato plants had to be carefully examined.

June found us cutting the grass in the field behind the pub for silage making. We had rather better quality grass that year and produced an even better silage. Unfortunately Rose now knew what the smell of molasses meant and she attacked the silo with her horns, finally tearing the sisalkraft paper. Then she dug a horn in and hooked out some silage. So stakes and barbed wire went round the silo to protect it.

One day, when I was getting a truss of hay from Frank's barn, I uncovered a family of three kittens. We knew they had been born, but had failed to find them. They were all ginger, one dark, one pale and one which was off-white with a very faint ginger-coloured pattern. Frank wanted to get rid of them and I offered to have the dark male. I didn't dare turn up at home with a female cat! We still had the four tomcats and Muff, who was very old and thin. I took Ginger home when he was about eight weeks old and he spent the first week in my bedroom and at night he slept on my pillow. Mum was not very pleased but he was a beautifully clean kitten with not a flea to be seen. On the ninth night he went outside and met the other cats. They took to him at once, and he curled up with Chat, who was about six months old. When my father found we had yet another cat he was not very pleased. Ginger, having spent a week in the house, regarded himself as a possible house cat. So began a running battle between him and Pa, which lasted until Ginger died, seven years later.

In June a near disaster struck: my father's ducks vanished. We were sure our local fox had had a hand in their disappearance, but there was nothing to prove he had been anywhere near them. A week later they all returned, fit and well. They quacked and waddled their way up the drive to the front door, in line astern behind the drake (there was only one by now – we had eaten the other). We never knew where they had been, how they

Treading the grass to pack it down.

had got out, or, for that matter, how they got in again.

My mother acted promptly and did as instructed by my father. She phoned his office and left a message with his secretary: "The ducks are back." He had insisted that if they did return, he should be told at once. We were sure they had gone for good, and were thinking of buying him some more. Pa's secretary acted equally promptly and phoned the Ministry of Agriculture, where he was attending a meeting of some sort. Whoever took the message had a sense of humour. He wrote it on a piece of paper, folded it in half and, entering the room discreetly, tiptoed up and handed it to my father. There was silence as he read the message.

"No bad news I hope?" the chairman asked anxiously.

"No, indeed, thank you. It is very good news," replied my father as he folded the paper and placed it in his wallet. A silence followed.

"Well, come on, tell us!" said the chairman.

"My ducks have been missing for a week," said Pa, enjoying every minute of it. "Half an hour ago they walked back up the drive to the front door."

During the summer Frank had a blind horse for a short time. We named him Dobbin and I drove him on several occasions. It was touching the trust that horse put in mere human beings. He had been blind from birth so had no idea what awful things lay in wait to frighten him, unlike young Kitty who, I was sure, felt the world was against her. He never shied, would go anywhere and do anything. He was gentle and very obedient but there was one great drawback: he was always in danger of hurting himself.

The first time I drove him we were haymaking in a very rough old paddock with a huge oak tree in the middle of it. The branches game down so low that they could catch Dobbin's head, and sweep me off the rake too! It meant getting down and leading him under the tree, and I had to pull his head down to miss the branches. The ground was uneven and had the odd rabbit hole as well, so I had to keep a sharp look out for anything he was likely to trip over, or put his hoof down .

As he never shied, I liked driving him on the road, but he had to be driven all the time or the nearside wheel would be in danger of going into the gutter, or up onto the bank. A sighted horse knew how far out to keep from the kerb. I felt sorry for him. He was only six years old, strong and loveable. One Monday I arrived for work to find that Dobbin had been sold to a costermonger in London. The amazing thing was the chap didn't realise for ages that his horse was blind. He obviously never let Dobbin do anything on his own, unlike the milkman's horse, which would usually move on to the next house.

One of the biggest bugbears for farmers during the war was double summer time. It upset us most during haymaking and harvest time. With the clock forward two hours we frequently couldn't begin picking up the hay until eleven o'clock, and occasionally as late as noon, so we would begin the day by doing odd jobs and there were always plenty of those!

I remember one day we were on a farm in Sarratt. There had been a particularly heavy dew and the sun was struggling to get through a heat haze. It was eventually going to be a very hot day, but though the hay had dried well the day before, the dew hadn't helped matters. I was driving the hay turner while the others were tossing the hay with pitchforks. At noon we began collecting in the hay from the middle of the field, where it was thinner. Round the outside it was still damp and I stayed on the turner until five o'clock, and then I went home to milk Frank's cow and deal with my animals. At eleven that night, I heard them returning. When we were working locally I very often went back to help them finish off a field, after dealing with my animals and having a bite to eat. Clearing up in the dark had its problems. The horses and dogs could see quite well, but hunting for the stray pitchforks and rescuing our bike from the hedge could be a problem. We worked very long hours in the summer because we still got up at the same time!

It was the beginning of August that Rose was served by a magnificent Guernsey bull, which lived at Mill Farm, down by the river at Chenies. Rose and I walked there and back, and it took us the best part of a day, allowing for rests every now and then. We set off at about nine o'clock on a day that promised to be blisteringly hot. I had sandwiches and some squash to keep me going. Rose had had a bigger breakfast than usual, and she would also have the chance of some grass on the way. We were using footpaths as much as possible, to cut down the mileage. Luckily Rose was easy to lead on a halter – in fact to begin with she was leading me, as she strode out. Every bit of lush grass was a terrible temptation to her and there were one or two battles when she found clover, which all cows love. Fortunately I was able to get a drink of water for her at one house, and taking a short cut through a field led us past a trough. So she wasn't doing too badly. We stopped for a breather after about three miles. I had my sandwiches and Rose ate grass.

The hill down into the Chess Valley is steep and winding, and I made the discovery that, unlike horses, cows do not have a braking instinct. Rose did not shorten her stride: she attacked the hill head on and began to

*Phillips mixing the molasses and water to spray
on the compacted grass.*

go faster as the hill took over. I feared she would fall because every now and then she tripped. The only way to deal with her was to tack from side to side, which seemed a stupid way to go down a hill, but the silly animal would not slow down. She was puffing and blowing by the time we reached the bottom and I was a bit out of breath myself. Steering Rose had been hard work! We walked to the farm, so beautifully situated in the little valley, with the river running through the fields. Mr Fitch met us and suggested we should both have a rest. Rose was put in a stable, given a bite to eat and plenty of water. I went into the house for some excellent homemade cakes and cold water. Wonderful after my tepid squash! Restored, we then met the bull, a magnificent animal, but he was light brown rather than Rose's golden brown, and parting the hairs at the end of his tail revealed a pale skin rather than the buttercup yellow of Rose's. Fortunately Rose also thought he was a handsome animal and was successfully mated. Then she was taken back to the stable for another rest and I was taken to see a six-month-old bull, who would one day take over from the old fellow. Mr Fitch admired Rose very much and said he would like to buy her calf if it was a heifer.

When we finally left it was hotter than ever. We plodded slowly up the hill with Rose stopping to munch at anything tasty. She found the hill tiring and was not very pleased. Several times she turned to glare at me and moo'd her displeasure.

However, once we were at the top she came to life and strode away at a much better pace. She had another drink from the trough, and further on a woman standing in a garden offered her a bucket of water, which Rose emptied gratefully. I don't remember what time it was when we finally reached home, but I know we were both weary. Naturally Rose was down on her milk yield that evening, but there was enough for the two calves and a bit for our breakfast.

During September I was on loan to Woodmans Farm where, the weather being fine, they were going to thresh from the stook. Before the war Boughtons had threshed from August to December, doing it from the stook whenever the weather permitted. I was delighted, and rushed off happily, thinking how nice it would be to see the Fowler earlier than usual. Imagine my dismay to find they were using a tractor! An ordinary, paraffin-driven, evil-smelling, large, bright yellow, American-built, Allis Chalmers tractor. I couldn't believe my eyes. It wasn't T T Boughtons' set after all. It was sacrilege and I never spent two such miserable days' threshing. I even got hay fever before I reached home. In fact I sneezed on and off all afternoon. I was not doing cavings clearing – I was helping to load the wagons in the fields. The drum had a blower for the cavings and they were in a neat pile at the side of it. One thing I did notice: the dust was much less because the corn was fresh.

Unfortunately it was true that some tractors did actually manage better than a traction engine. It goes against the grain to say it, but the Watt governors on some steam engines were not all that good, while governors on some tractors were very efficient. Some farmers would ask the driver to leave the traction engine idle and would hitch up their own tractor to the drum because they objected to the price of coal, which they had to provide, or said they had none to spare on the farm. The traction engine drivers resented this very much. They were proud of their engines and hated to see them standing idle.

I sympathised with the drivers. The traction engines found a place in people's hearts and were lovingly cared for by most of the men who worked with them. To get the best out of the engines they had to be properly cared for and maintenance had to be carried out on a regular basis. One of the not so popular jobs was the boiler wash out. If they were steamed for more than 100 to 150 hours without a thorough wash out, the water would foam and froth, due to impurities in it. There was a good chance it would get into the valves and cylinders. Water cannot be compressed, so its presence in the wrong place could lead to a bent rod, or a blown-out cylinder cover.

Engines very often had to fill up from ponds and as these were usually inhabited by ducks and used by cattle, the water was far from clean, so a build-up of sludge round the base of the firebox was a common hazard. A furred-up engine would not steam very well and would burn more coal.

At Boughtons the drivers were encouraged to do the wash out in the evenings when the engines were still fairly warm, or on Sundays. For this task they were paid a few extra shillings. Most drivers took great pride in looking after their engines really well, but just occasionally there would be the driver who said he had done the wash out when he hadn't, and some engines were ruined this way and had to have new fireboxes.

Retubing was done every six or seven years. Some contractors removed the tubes every year to descale them, but not Boughtons. Travelling about as they did, they were using all sorts of water – some hard, some soft. If hard water had to be used most of the time, then water treatment as well as boiler wash outs would be part of the routine.

Every year the crew that had put in the most "belt hours" would receive a prize. 2000 hours was the top score and among the older men it was usually about 700. At their peak Boughtons were covering 750 farms a year. One farm was so big that the threshing set spent nearly a whole year there, dealing with corn from 1000 acres. One or two other sets covered the slightly smaller farms and would probably manage four farms a year. The rest did the small farms such as the ones we helped on. Didi Hobbs and Bill Harris were among the top crews and had one of the best-kept engines.

With more and more land being ploughed up for cereals, T T Boughton found themselves with considerably more threshing to do. It was essential to increase the number of sets and by 1943 they had fifteen. This had been made possible by buying up old traction engines, most of which were derelict; and threshing drums, which had become redundant after the First World War, when so much land went back to grass.

The drums had very often been used as hen houses or just left to rot. Boughtons bought them and in two months their carpenters had rebuilt them. Luckily it was still possible to buy the other parts, such as beaters, corn screens and elevator cups. Then the Government commandeered thirty sets from an old firm of contractors which had closed down. The brothers who ran it were both over eighty years old and had decided to retire. Boughtons took over ten of their sets.

Before the war one set had managed to do all the threshing from Bushey in Herts to Great Missenden in Bucks – about fourteen miles. During the war so much grassland had been ploughed up that fifteen sets were needed to cover the same area. We worked with the same set every year and finally Didi and Bill became used to a girl working with them.

Several times I had said I would like to help with thatching if ever the opportunity arose. It was towards the end of August that my wish was granted. We had just gathered in a large field of wheat and Jim had been asked to thatch it as quickly as possible. So I found myself being instructed in the art of "yealming". Yealms are best described as straw tiles, and making them is a back-breaking job! First Jim had to estimate how many yealms he needed per "laddering" (one row up the stack). Trusses of long straw were laid out (the butt or cut end towards you), the twine holding them together was cut and removed, water was sprinkled on them and a good heavy plank laid across them. This was to keep them in place when the straw was pulled out for making yealms. You started at the end of the line of straw and pulled it up your legs, packing it tightly and combing it with your fingers to remove loose bits. When the yealm stretched from your thighs to your ankles and was of the right thickness, you laid it on the twine, lying ready on the ground. You alternated them so they made an "X", and tied them with the twine.

When you ran out of straw you pulled out more and worked your way along the line again. Each yealm was kept in place on the rick with rick pegs, which were long and thin and were driven far into the corn rick or haystack and tied in place by twine from peg to peg. Jim showed me how to split the wood to make the pegs, which looked easy but I found it difficult to follow the grain of the wood, so mine turned out to be half the length. I only made one!

Jim would start at the eaves of the hay or corn and worked his way up. Each yealm overlapped the one below it so the rain would run down the straw and not into it. It took a lot of straw, pegs and twine to securely thatch a rick. This is a very simple description. It was a lengthy job and could not be rushed but at the end there would be a beautifully thatched haystack or corn rick. Jim was a very good thatcher and I loved helping him. He said I made good yealms!

At the end of the year Phillips was called up. We were sorry to see him go: he had been with us for about nine years and under his care the garden, both flower and vegetable, had flourished. He had helped with the rabbits and no end of other jobs and it would be very difficult to find a suitable replacement. Fortunately, through the Home Guard, my father was put in touch with Tom Stevens. He was the same age as Pa, and a countryman born and bred who reckoned he could do most of the jobs. He looked at the plough, grinning all over his face, and said he could do far better with a spade, and probably as quickly too, he reckoned. He couldn't be with us full time, but he managed to put in enough hours a week to keep things going. Mum had feared she would have to get rid of the rabbits, but by rearranging the timetable she was able to keep them. Phillips had always helped to clean the hutches every day, but by making it an early evening job I could do them after milking. Tom did the killing and skinning and Mum continued to do the gutting. It all worked out quite well and the rabbits stayed on until 1946. The hens were easy as they were free range and there wouldn't be any more cockerels for fattening until next spring.

Shorn sheep and their lambs penned on the lawn.

In the *Farmer and Stockbreeder* I read an article about the advantages of ploughing up old grassland and sowing it with oats and mixed grasses – the idea being that the oats would act as a shield for the young grass, and it would be cut before it was ripe, for silage or hay. The grasses would grow and be ready for light grazing, probably in July. By the following year there should be a good pasture, or alternatively, it could be closed for hay. It was a way of improving worn-out grazing. It seemed a good idea, and I decided to ask Frank to plough up the top half of the meadow in December, ready for planting towards the end of March. I was sure the field would be greatly improved. It was old pasture and in spite of harrowing to remove dead grass and spreading the dung, and making sure Rose and Sue grazed it together, it had not improved. So drastic measures were necessary.

Horses are very bad grazers and only eat the best grass, which they graze far too short, so Rose always had to graze with Sue. For the same reason, she had to join the sheep in the orchard, when we had them, to eat up the bits they left. Rose regarded wilted nettles as a delicacy so we cut the clump in the orchard regularly, to feed her. The same applied to wilted thistles, and milk thistles.

Unfortunately she managed to poison herself by eating hemlock. I found a miserable, groaning, dribbling Rose lying by the orchard gate. I sent for the vet, Mr Barr. "Hemlock poisoning," he said, as soon as he saw her. He had a magical drench to give her, which was the colour of cold tea, and by the next morning she was back to her old self. I had never thought of looking for hemlock and a thorough search of the orchard revealed it, down by the drive gates, growing between the pond and the wall. There were only a few plants but they were huge and looked very like cow parsley. I was surprised that the nasty dank smell of the plants hadn't put Rose off. We dug them all up and had no more trouble.

The goldfish, which had flourished in the pond before the war, had now all disappeared. They had been very big ones and we didn't think the ducks could have eaten them, but we did wonder about the tomcat called Nervous. There was a flight of three small steps down to the water's edge, and that was where he used to sit. No one ever saw him catch a fish but the evidence seemed to point to him. So we did not restock the pond.

It was potato-lifting time again and we began with Frank's meagre crop, and then moved on to an enormous one at a farm near Flaunden. We asked the farmer if we could build a bonfire and cook some potatoes in it for our lunch. He very kindly agreed and showed us where we could get some dead wood from a small coppice. Jim started the fire and we grabbed some large potatoes from the first ridge, which George had split open. We cleaned them on an old sack and once the fire was burning well the potatoes were put at the bottom. During the morning we took it in turns to tend the fire. By lunchtime there were a dozen well-charred potatoes to be dragged clear and left to cool for a moment or two. Pocket knives were produced and we all dug happily into wonderful baked potatoes. They were a great treat and tasted very good.

The marrow-stem kale was now supposed to be ready for cutting, for winter feed. It had not grown all that well in spite of the top dressing it had received earlier in the year, and looked much more like thousand-headed kale. However, Rose thought it was succulent and scrunched her way happily through the lot. It was not going to last her as long as I had hoped, so it was just as well we had filled the gaps with cabbages. They were big, thanks, no doubt, to the generous dollop of manure under each one.

In the extension vegetable garden we had planted thousand-headed and curly kale; the usual long line of artichokes; and plenty of carrots, turnips and swedes. Apart from an early attack of the flea beetle everything had done well. Phillips had never used any top dressings in the vegetable garden. Soot was put along the onion rows but otherwise he relied entirely on plenty of good compost.

In December the top half of the meadow was ploughed. George made a very good job of it and buried the old grass completely. It was left to weather until the end of February and then I attacked it with old Kitty and the scuffles. It was hard and unyielding and did not break down as well as I had expected. Next I used the tine harrows and produced a tilth, of sorts. I was disappointed and a bit concerned because I knew that if the ground was not right I would end up with a poor crop of grass. In March I sowed the oats first, to act as the nurse crop. I dressed it against the fungal diseases, using a terribly brightly coloured chemical which I think was mercuric oxide, or some such poisonous substance. I remember mixing the oats and the dressing in a huge bucket to make sure every grain was well covered. I didn't wear gloves and I must have breathed in some of the powder, it was so fine. But in those days we were not as aware of the potential dangers of chemical farming as we are now. I broadcast the grain and luckily no one was watching! The oats were harrowed in and then a few days later I sowed the grass, using Frank's seed barrow. I had been advised to use a mixture suitable for heavy soils and seem to remember that it included perennial rye grass, cocksfoot, Timothy grass, rough-stalked meadow grass and two clovers. No doubt it would have also had its share of weeds, thistles and nettles, which always appeared as if by magic! Then the chain harrow was taken over it very carefully, and finally the ring roller. A week later it was rolled again to compact it as much as possible. All that was needed was some rain, some warmth and lots of luck.

During the winter Neda had been taken ill. Mr Barr diagnosed cancer and, sadly, we lost our other mastiff. She had been a most affectionate animal, desolate without Cosmo, on whom she depended, but she did not have his character and, compared with him, was a bit dim. He was unkind to her and bullied her. She was not the love of his life by any means: it was the puppy called Ruby who had won his heart. She was a Christmas present to Mum in 1936, and was an eight-month-old mastiff puppy. I shall never forget the day she arrived. It was Christmas Eve and Pa said he had to go out and collect something. He took John with him. They were away for ages, it began to snow, and Mum and I were beginning to get bothered. Suddenly the lounge door opened and in galloped Ruby. She had beautiful dark-brown eyes which sparkled with fun, and she rushed up to Mum and leapt up to lick her. Then she greeted Cosmo with a lick on his nose, a big wag of her tail, and climbed onto a chair. It all happened in seconds and for Cosmo it was love at first sight. She used to pinch his place by the fire and he would move away without a murmur. If he tried to sit beside her she would growl at him. She stole his food and he never complained. She played with him in the garden and teased him mercilessly. She was all puppy; he was four years old. When she was being particularly tiresome he would look at Mum as though to say, "She is adorable and can do no wrong." His eyes spoke volumes and when a year later she died from distemper, he was distraught.

It seemed bleak without Neda; and Mum, for some inexplicable reason, went from the sublime to the ridiculous and bought a wire-haired terrier. Paddy was so small in comparison that we frequently trod on him or fell over him. Poor Paddy: he must have wondered what was the matter with us. The cats were surprised, and not a little cross. Paddy plagued them and there was a veritable chorus of growling, hissing and spitting from all of them whenever Paddy went into the barn. He finally made friends with the Old English buck rabbit, and the two would play a game.

When the rabbits had their cages cleaned the buck was put on the ground to have a hop around. He was very tame and easy to catch, so Mum thought a bit of exercise would do him no harm. One day Paddy wandered into the barn and watched the buck as he hopped round the big cages on the floor. Paddy went quietly round in the opposite direction and waited at the end of the row for the buck to come round the corner. When he did, the two animals bumped noses. The buck was genuinely surprised, jumped in the air, turned and went the other way. Paddy waited for him at the next corner, and sure enough the same thing happened. They bumped noses, the buck jumped, turned round and hopped away. It became their standard game and they played it nearly every day until Mum got rid of the rabbits. I wish I had taken a photograph of the cats watching it all from a safe perch. Disbelief was registered on each face.

It was interesting to see the reactions of Sue, Rose and Jersey to the arrival of Paddy. Being a terrier he feared nothing, and he would get dangerously near to Rose's horns. She would put her head down and run at him. He would skip aside as she galumphed past. He was naughty and had many a spank until he learned to leave her alone. Jersey, that timid calf, backed away from him and he tried nipping her heels. The spank he got for that put him off for good. Sue had her own remedy: he came up behind her one day and she lashed out, luckily missing him. He never tried that again. So all animals and humans settled down with the tiny dog and found him to be a most intelligent and happy companion.

Then someone suggested we should buy a bull-mastiff and Rufus joined us. That was a big mistake. Once more little dog led big dog astray and they were always getting out and disappearing for half a day. We were most concerned because Rufus, though nothing like as large as a mastiff, was a strong dog and he could have killed sheep or chased cows. It was most fortunate that he had a fear of cows and was not interested in sheep. We knew from reported sightings that the two dogs roamed far and wide, and they would arrive back plastered in mud and worn out. Poor Rufus! I think Paddy ran him off his feet.

During the spring of 1944 I couldn't keep my eyes off the top half of the meadow, where I hoped the oats and grasses would soon appear. The other great excitement was the prospect of Rose having a heifer calf. By the middle of March she had been dried off, as this time I wanted her to have at least ten weeks in which to build up her strength for the pedigree calf she was carrying. Even if it was a bull, it would be worth keeping – someone might be interested in a good pedigree Guernsey. The calves had been sold, and I was again buying a few pints of milk from Frank. I had decided that I would not buy a calf to keep the new one company – instead I would try my hand at making cheese. I had read another encouraging article, this time in *The Smallholder*. If only they didn't make everything sound so easy!

I had been making ordinary curd cheese on and off ever since Rose arrived, but now I would try my hand at hard cheeses. All I had to do was let the required amount of milk stand overnight in the warm, increase the temperature the next morning, then add rennet; then when a junket had formed, cut it into squares, cook it, strain off the whey, pack it into containers, put weights on top and leave it to ripen. It really did sound easy. I was sure I would succeed.

In preparation for the latest experiment, Pa bought me two large enamel bins, which would have the hot water in them; two smaller enamel bins, which would fit inside and contain the milk; and a thermometer. I even managed to get some cheesecloth. In Watford I found just the right sized cake tins, with loose bottoms, in which to pack the curd. A good hunt in both barns revealed all sorts of heavy bits and pieces to act as weights. I was not going to have a cheese press. All we needed was for Rose to calve, then family and friends would be receiving nice small cheeses to eke out the ration.

Before that great day arrived there were all the many spring jobs to do, so I had to forget about cheese making and concentrate on the job of planning what was to be planted for the next winter. Tom scorned the little plough and dug all the top of the orchard by himself. He dug in manure – lots of it. He even made me buy some more, because he had been so disgusted with the size of the marrow-stem kale.

I tried ploughing the extension vegetable patch by myself. It was no good: Sue couldn't, or wouldn't go straight. So I had to get John to lead her. During the previous year Phillips had weighted the plough with a large lump of lead he discovered in the barn. It made all the difference and, though Sue had to work a bit harder, we did get a reasonable furrow. Tom was most amused but at least he didn't have to dig that bit as well. The kale was sown a month earlier than in 1943, and with all that manure it should be tall and strong.

Chapter Six

Just after the war started, my father bought an old car trailer for the Home Guard. He equipped it with a stirrup pump, and a huge asbestos bell-shaped contraption with a handle. This was for dropping on top of incendiary bombs. We reckoned that for the bell to be effective it needed to be put over the bomb as it landed, so as to cover it up before it set fire to anything. He also bought a shovel and a quantity of sand. In those early days firefighting practice was carried out every Sunday. Things were set alight in various fields and the Home Guard would come running, with the trailer, to put out the fire. Had they tried dropping the cover over a real incendiary bomb, I think someone would have been seriously burnt. We even set fire to some straw outside an unoccupied hen house to see how quickly it could be put out using the stirrup pump. I had put one of my dolls inside to represent the occupant. The doll survived and still exists. We all knew the exercises were futile, because the equipment was totally inadequate, but at least we all felt something was being done, and those exercises definitely helped to mould the Home Guard. Finally, the trailer was needed no more and we kept it, and the stirrup pump, in the barn for our own use.

Home Guard stories abound: it really was like "Dad's Army" and one we all enjoyed was the day Kings Langley had to "invade" Chipperfield. It was a return match and Kings Langley were out for revenge! Chipperfield had taken them by surprise the previous weekend. For ages no one could discover where the Kings Langley platoon had got to. They hadn't been sighted and time was going by. Jim had been sent up a tree in one of the fields opposite our house. He was sitting there, scanning the countryside and feeling a bit bored, when he noticed one of Mrs Martin's cows turn its head and stare at the hedge. It began to walk slowly down the field. Several other cows followed it, then they stopped and all of them stared at the hedge. It was very thick and on the other side was a footpath leading to Scatterdells Lane, which was parallel with ours. Jim watched the cows for a moment longer as they turned their heads slowly to follow the progress of whatever was the other side of the hedge. As quickly as he could he scrambled down the tree and ran up the lane, to alert other members of the platoon. He was pretty sure it was the Kings Langley "enemy", who had managed to evade the traps laid for them. Jim and the others reached the footpath just as the enemy was crawling out into the lane. They were captured and the whole herd of cows had come down the field to witness it. Every now and then a senior officer from Eastern Command would inspect the Home Guard. The platoon would be lined up on Chipperfield Common, all looking as spick and span as possible, with polished boots and clean rifles. On one occasion Jim had decided to have a little sport in the woods before the parade. He put his ferret in his gas mask case. On this occasion the senior officer decided to do a random inspection of gas masks. Jim's heart was in his mouth but luckily his "gas mask" was not checked and equally luckily, the ferret was quite quiet and still.

Early in 1944 I asked Pa if I could have shafts put on the trailer to make another cart. The resulting peculiar-looking vehicle was very useful for carting things round our smallholding and, to our surprise, it also proved to be reasonably comfortable to ride in. One Sunday in March we decided to try it out. My father had recently recovered from an attack of pneumonia and was out and about again, but he would not be on parade with the Home Guard until the following Sunday.

Ma and Pa sat at the back on two very small, low, folding picnic chairs, with a big thick car rug wrapped round them. John and I sat in front of them on a plank which fitted across the trailer, and was fixed so it would not slide backwards or forwards. It was peculiar to drive because

Cosmo and Neda in the open barn.

you were low down and couldn't see over the horse. So I drove, watching out for oncoming traffic, and John kept an eye on the near side. It caused a stir, unsurprisingly, for we looked quite daft. Sue found it easy to pull and set off at a spanking pace. She was a good trotter and we shot off towards Bovingdon. At the crossroads we turned left for Flaunden, with a view to visiting the pub at Hoggspit Bottom. No one noticed us when we arrived. I tied Sue to a convenient post and we went in to get warm in front on the fire and have a drink. While we were enjoying the cosy atmosphere a customer came in.

"Whose is the mare outside?" he asked. "She's backed that extraordinary vehicle partly into the road." That did it. Everyone in the pub had to go to the windows to look outside.

"What on earth is it?" asked several of the locals. Pa explained.

"You ride in that?" they exclaimed incredulously.

"We tried it out today," I said, "but normally I use it for carting things round our smallholding – manure, for example – but," I added hastily, "it was scrubbed out before we rode in it."

When we finally left everyone turned out to see us off. They watched as we got Ma and Pa settled in the back, with the rug wrapped round them. I climbed in next, while John unhitched Sue. He was going to drive home. We left smartly from the forecourt, to rousing cheers, and headed for Belsize.

The lane was narrow and twisty and I wished Sue had been fitted with a horn. Standing up in a cart gave a better chance of seeing what was ahead. Sitting low down staring at the hindquarters of a horse made me feel vulnerable. However, we did not meet much and, fortunately, in those days people didn't drive at quite such breakneck speeds round the lanes. We reached Belsize and turned left for Chipperfield. There were people coming out of the pub and a cheer went up as we trotted past. Sue's ears did a bit of rapid semaphoring and she put on a spurt. Pa waved in a dignified manner.

We reached the next crossroads by the grocer's shop and yet another pub, where, of course, there was more cheering. We turned left and up the short steep hill, then trotted up the shallow incline to Frank's farm. Right turn, and we were in our lane leading to the house. It had been an amusing outing, and we had all enjoyed it. The next day Frank said, grinning broadly, "I saw you coming back from your Sunday ride!"

The following Sunday Pa was back with the Home Guard. One of our friends from up the road told him he had seen us trotting past. He had

yelled to his wife, "Bring my hunting horn, quickly." She had been unable to get upstairs fast enough, so he had missed the chance of giving us a
fanfare. Just as well. I think Sue would have had a fit on hearing a horn at
such close quarters.

Spring was here and with it all the sowing, harrowing and rolling.
Lots of days were spent walking up and down behind either the tine harrows or the roller. It was peaceful: no sounds except the songs of the birds,
the jangle of harness, the squeaking and creaking of the roller and the
scraping of the harrows. It was a good life and I was glad Frank did not
have a tractor. In our area, several of the bigger farms now had tractors
and they did make some jobs easier. Potato lifting was one for which they
did not seem suitable. During the previous autumn we had helped with
the potato harvest at Woodmans Farm. There, a Fordson tractor pulling
a spinner had galloped over the field. It didn't take so long to collect the
potatoes, because most of them were exposed, which wasn't always the
case with the ridging plough, but the amount of damage was extensive,
which must have made the crop an expensive one.

It was at Woodmans Farm that I first saw a milking parlour. It was
a novel invention but many of the cows refused to change from hand- to
machine-milking, and would kick the cups off. Some cows could even be
devils to milk by hand, and one story Frank told me concerned a young,
wild-looking, jet-black cow that had just had her first calf. No one seemed
able to milk her, so Frank bought her. He had an obliging calf which managed to suck a quantity of milk from her without being kicked uncon-
scious, so that solved the immediate problem.

Frank knew an old chap with a "peg leg" who had asked him to look
out for a quiet cow. He stressed that it must be quiet as he was no longer
nimble. He also had a reputation for being able to handle difficult animals,
so Frank sold him the black cow. He told him it was quiet and wondered
what would happen! A week later the old chap saw Frank and told him she
was the best milker he had ever had and he was delighted with her. She
lived to a ripe old age and never gave him a moment's trouble, but no one
else could ever milk her.

In April we realised just how much damage Frank had done to our
raspberries the previous winter. He and Jim had very kindly offered to
come and do a bit of pruning to the old apple trees, and Mum had gratefully accepted. When Frank had finished helping Jim in the orchard, he
went looking for more things to trim. Unfortunately he was armed with
a sickle, usually referred to as a bagging hook. Phillips used to do all the

Cosmo.

pruning, but since his departure we had got behind and the raspberries had not been touched. Unfortunately Frank noticed them and went into the attack with his sickle, just to tidy them up, he said. Jim nearly had a fit when he saw the result. Most of the new growth had gone. Frank apologised to Mum and said Mrs Pritchard never allowed him to prune the soft fruit. Mum, on looking at the devastation, replied that she could understand why! The 1944 crop was very poor and Frank did not offer to trim our raspberries again.

Every day I examined the top half of the meadow, looking for any signs of the grass or oats. When they did eventually appear the oats were so few and far between that there was no point in cutting them for silage. The grass wasn't all that plentiful to begin with either. A top dressing of sulphate of ammonia did help and Frank reckoned that by next summer there would be a good crop. Rose and the calves would graze it for a few hours each day from about August onwards, and that would strengthen the grass. Then it would be closed for hay in 1945.

At last it was time for Rose to have her calf. The suspense had been killing me. I was sure it would arrive on a weekday, when I was at work, but luck was with me this time, and she calved on a Saturday afternoon. It was my uncle and aunt, in the cottage, who first heard her mooing. My aunt came over to tell me. I rushed out to make sure all was well and arrived a few moments before the calf was born. Rose always calved easily and this one was no exception. It was a big calf but, to my delight, at last we had a heifer! She was the image of her mother, with the same white triangle on her face. Quickly I helped Rose remove the membrane from the calf's head so that it could breathe more easily, and Rose began to lick her. But, to my dismay, the calf lay on its side with its head back, as though it had given up. It made no attempt to lift its head. Rose stopped licking it, sniffed it and then turned away. To her the signs were of a calf about to die, and she was not going to bother with it. She began eating the afterbirth, and I bent down, picked the calf up, all wet and very slippery, and rushed as fast as I could to the barn. Luckily I had not shut the gate when I went into the meadow so I left it open, hoping Rose would follow me. But her calf was not making any noise and Rose was sure it was dead.

Luckily my father came out of the back door as I shot into the open barn.

"Quick," I said, as I put the calf down. "Please could you get a bale of straw from the big barn while I hold the calf's head up? I've got to prop it up or it will die." Pa fetched the straw and we leant the calf against the bale so that it couldn't lie on its side. It was breathing quite normally but looked dopey.

I rubbed it hard with straw to dry it and stimulate the blood flow. My beautiful heifer must live. There wasn't any time to lose. Next I rushed back to get Rose, who was standing where I had left her. She bent down and sniffed the ground, obviously still remembering her calf. Luckily I smelt strongly of calf – in fact the whole of my front was wet. Rose sniffed me as I stood in front of her. Then she mooed.

"Come on, Rose," I shouted, getting behind her to drive her out of the field. "I want milk for your calf." Rose walked slowly ahead of me and I finally got her into the open barn with her calf. She went over to it, sniffed it and licked it a bit, but still it did not moo. I tied Rose up at the manger and shot into the kitchen for the milking bucket. I must get some milk into that calf. Rose parted with several pints of colostrum and I poured it into the calf feeder. I managed to get the teat into the calf's mouth but it wouldn't suck. Despair was setting in. I removed the rubber ball that acted as a valve and let some milk pour down the calf's throat. It gulped. I lifted the ball again; more milk went down. I was afraid it would choke if I let it have too much all at once. I hadn't the faintest idea how much milk I should give it. All the previous calves had been able to look after themselves and had been up on their feet in no time at all. This one showed no sign of wanting to get up. It took a little more milk and then I decided to see if it could stand. I removed the bale and it fell onto its side, head back again. I gritted my teeth. "I am not going to lose this calf," I said to the two cats who were watching. Again I propped the calf up and went into the house to get some help.

As Rose was safely tied up Mum was quite happy to assist me, but first I must give poor Rose a drink. She was probably very thirsty, and hungry, but she would have to wait a bit longer for a feed. Rose drank all the water and then I returned to the problem of the calf. Mum and I rubbed it with straw. We did its legs, its body and rolled it over to do the same the other side. We rubbed and rubbed, until our arms ached. Suddenly it shook its head, sneezed and said, "Moo." Rose mooed back and turned to look at her calf. At last she was showing interest. We tried to get the calf up on its feet, and after several attempts we succeeded. It was very wobbly but it was standing. It fell down and we propped it up again with the bale, but it didn't really need it and seemed much more alert. It lay on the ground, looking in the direction of Rose, and mooed several times! We were so pleased – at last the calf looked as though it would survive. I decided I had better feed Rose, and Mum stayed with the calf while I went off to mix up a good brew. I gave Rose two pounds of molasses mixed in three pints of warm water, and a warm bran mash, pinched from the rabbits' rations!

At last the calf was taking an interest in its surroundings, so I gave it some more milk. Its next feed would be from Rose. I decided to make a pen out of four bales of straw to keep it warm and to prevent it lying on its side. Also I bathed the umbilical cord with disinfectant and applied Stockholm tar, just in case there was any likelihood of "navel ill". I had had no trouble with Rose's previous calves and was certain we did not have the bacteria on our land, but with the beautiful pedigree heifer I was not taking any risks.

It had taken two hours to deal with the calf and it was time to attend to the other animals. We were late feeding the rabbits, who were all hopping back and forth in their cages. The hens were crowded round the hen run gate, clucking their disgust, and five cats were lined up waiting for a drink of milk. Even Whisky had deserted his seat on top of the hatchway in the kitchen.

By nine o'clock the calf was standing up without wobbling, and I decided to move her and Rose into the big barn and bed them down for the night. The calf would definitely survive. She had another feed, from Rose this time, and needed no help. I took one last look at them, before I went to bed. They were lying down, warm and happy. Next day I telephoned Mr Fitch with the good news and we christened the calf Rosemary.

Now that the great cheese experiment was about to begin I decided to use Meadow View as my cheese room. John's trains had been removed long ago and we now stored apples, bottled tomatoes, and also some bottled chicken on the shelves. Then we read an article warning us against the bottling of chicken. We could be poisoned. It was fed to the dogs and I was not very pleased. Cooking and bottling eight large Light Sussex cockerels had taken me ages. We also stored marrows in muslin, hanging them from the ceiling. One burst and made the most awful mess.

Meadow View was scrubbed down, disinfected and the walls were whitewashed. Then it was aired for a week and at last I was ready to begin. The cheese had to be made at the weekend as it was obviously going to take all day. I began with a gallon of Friday evening's milk and left it in the kitchen so that it would not be too cold. First thing on Saturday morning it was poured into a one-gallon enamel can, which was put into a large enamel bin containing hot water. The temperature of the milk had to be gently raised to about eighty-six degrees Fahrenheit and then rennet was added to set the milk in a junket. The time for this varied and the temperature of the water surrounding the container had to be tested regularly and more hot water added as necessary, to maintain the curd at about eighty-six degrees. It meant bailing out some water and pouring more in.

After about an hour the curd was usually ready for cutting into cubes. I had no curd knives, which would cut horizontally and vertically, and used a carving knife, so the curd was not in neat cubes. It was very gently stirred and then the temperature was slowly raised to about 100 degrees. To do this I removed the cheese container and stood it on the table, emptied the water from the large bin, and filled up with much hotter water. The thermometer was vital because the temperature had to rise slowly. If the curd was cooked quickly the results were awful. It was supposed to take an hour to reach 100 degrees, and I had a kettle of boiling water on the go, for topping up. It was a slow job and I didn't dare take my eyes off it.

When the hour was up the curd had to be stirred for five to ten minutes and then left to settle for about an hour. Then, with a slotted spoon I carefully lifted the curd out and put it into my milk strainer, lined with butter muslin, for it to drain well and harden. The next step was to pack the cold curd into the cake tins, which had been lined with butter muslin and were standing on a well-scrubbed board. The bottoms of the cake tins were put on top of the curd and the first weights put on. The cheeses were taken out to Meadow View and placed on the table. The next day the weights were increased to squeeze out the remaining whey.

When the cheeses had set well and no more whey was being squeezed out, I removed them from their tins, left the muslin on them and rubbed them with salt. They were then placed on a shelf and left to ripen – hopefully! I had intended leaving them for at least eight weeks; but after four, curiosity got the better of me and I had to cut one open. It was a total disaster, so I cut open the other two. They were the same. The smell was awful, like wet rot, and there was a mould inside which was some ferocious strain I had not seen before. There was nothing for it but to offer the offensive stuff to any animal that would eat it. I tried them all but every one of them wrinkled up their noses and backed away, so I cut the cheeses up and boiled the pieces along with the scraps for the hens. Mixed with mash they didn't know what they were eating.

My next attempt was more successful so, encouraged, I took to making cheese every week. I made quite a lot and several times produced a pleasantly flavoured, though rubbery-textured version of the real thing. I varied the number of weeks I kept each batch and found that twelve was the best. I still, occasionally, had a real disaster and I never discovered why. Family and friends found the cheese a useful addition to the ration, but it was not very good for cooking, though we sometimes used it for macaroni cheese, and ate it with baked potatoes. I also made cottage, or curd cheese, which my uncle loved and ate with sugar.

Haymaking time was upon us again and in 1944 Sue did a considerable amount of hay raking. She knew very well that when she worked for Frank she had a feed of oats and at the end of the day she would battle with me as we walked home, trying her hardest to get at the little sack of crushed oats. I liked driving her in the hayrake – she was very sensible and knew just what we had to do. She was also the only horse I ever trusted on the road with the hayrake. I have to admit I did everything I could to get out of driving the darned thing on the road. It was so wide that nothing could pass it, unless you took one wheel up onto the grass verge, or took refuge in a gateway. Some of the verges were quite high and the rake would be tilted sharply. Not all horses liked struggling to get it up on the verge, or the rattle and crash when it came down again, and I liked it even less, which all the horses knew! Sue, when working regularly, was calm and not bothered by difficulties, but even with Sue I hated taking the rake through a gate. It was a very close fit and I always got one or the other wheel hubs stuck against the gate post. No horse was happy if the vehicle it was pulling got

Rose and calf.

stuck, and would begin to prance. As I was no good with a prancing horse, I usually pleaded with someone to lead me into the field. The only horse I ever found easy was Dobbin: he couldn't see what was happening so he was not worried. With him I managed gates quite happily!

Rosemary was three months old and growing into a beautiful calf. Jersey enjoyed her company and the two were firm friends. Sometimes Rufus and Paddy played what looked like a game of tag with them. If they all got too close to Rose she would shake her horns, while Sue looked very menacing and snorted at them, ears flat and angry eyes. It was not only Rosemary who was growing at a pace; Jersey was becoming a beautiful young heifer and in about six months I would have to look for a suitable bull.

All the vegetables were coming on extremely well and a bumper crop of marrow-stem kale was growing in the strip at the top of the orchard. Tom was very pleased with himself and told me it was just as well he had insisted on lots of manure. It was harder work without Phillips but we were managing far better then any of us had expected.

Haymaking was progressing well and while the weather was fine Jim was away most days mowing the grass. Teddy, the collie, was always with him. Teddy hated thunder and knew when a storm was brewing. To attract

Jim's attention he would walk just in front of the horses, which worried them, so it was a good way of getting Jim's attention. It meant that in about an hour Teddy would shoot into the kitchen and sit shivering under the kitchen table until the storm was over. He was also gun-shy and always ran away, until one day Jim shot a rabbit, which managed to run a short distance straight into Teddy's mouth. From that day on Teddy stayed with Jim, in case it happened again!

Just occasionally I would be away hay raking by myself, preparing the field for the next day. This would happen if there was a long spell of fine weather, with everyone wanting their hay gathered in at the same time. With the fickle English weather this did not happen very often, but when it did we were hard-pressed to finish before the rain came. Sometimes the hayrake would be left ready in the field, so Sue and I only had to walk there. Other times I had to drive the rake from Frank's yard to the field in question and, coward that I was, hope and pray someone would take the rake in for me. Mostly I was lucky and someone would come to my rescue!

Several of the farmers preferred to store the hay in their barns, which meant carting it out of the fields in wagons and carts. The hay was picked up from the rows I had raked, and stacked up high on the wagons. My muscles had improved a great deal with all the work I had done, and I found I could pitch the hay quite well. Frank had found a small pitchfork in his barn and had given it to me in 1942.

"It's a ladies' pitchfork," he told me. "It can't pick up too much, so you'll find it easy to use." I thanked him and practised with it at home, before I ventured to do any pitching at haymaking and harvesting. The men could gather huge amounts of hay with their large pitchforks and toss it effortlessly up to the man on top, who was stacking it carefully to make a big, properly balanced load. There was nothing more tiresome than having to retrieve a load that had fallen off a cart or wagon.

When half the field had been cleared my job would be to collect the stray bits of hay with the hayrake. I did not rake it into rows, as I would do when we were sweeping the fields, but took it to the wagon. Frank used to take along his big wagon and his cart, with the "ladder" on. This was a frame, which fitted on to the front of the cart and protruded out over the horse. With the tailboard out flat (held in place by chains on either side), quite a big load of hay could be carried in an ordinary cart. Each farmer would use his carts as well, so we had a steady flow of hay going back to the barns, where the men would be stacking it.

I helped Jim build a haystack one day and it was not as difficult as I had imagined. Hay that is warm and dry is incredibly slippery and I succeeded in slipping off the stack! Luckily we were only about five feet off the ground, but I did feel an awful idiot. When building a haystack, the same rule applied as with a corn rick: it had to be slightly wider at the top than at the bottom, before tapering off. As an elevator was not used, a ladder would be placed against the stack when it was about six or seven feet high, and the pitchers below would carry the hay up the ladder to the builders. Before finishing the stack the sides were raked down to remove all the untidy loose bits of hay, which were then put on top. Everyone took great pride in building good, well-shaped haystacks and corn ricks, and always tried to thatch them better than anyone else. In those days nothing looked more pleasing than a group of well-built and well-thatched corn ricks or haystacks. The landscape looked more homely than it does now.

Frank's big eleven-acre field had been sown to wheat and there was a marvellous crop, helped no doubt by the lime and manure, which had been spread the previous year. Jim built a huge rick near the yard, so that it would be easy to get the threshing tackle up to it. I helped with the thatching and again it poured with rain. I think it took us two, if not three days to complete and I did feel a bit stiff after such a lengthy stint of yealming.

On our smallholding that year we had not made much hay and, just for fun, we built a small circular haystack. I was going to cover it with a huge tarpaulin, but Jim asked if he could thatch it as he had never tried a circular stack. He did a nice decorative topknot to finish it off. When the time came to cut into the stack, it seemed a shame to destroy the elegant decoration!

During harvesting I was stung, for the second time in my life, by several wasps. When George came round with the binder he disturbed the wasps and we had several flying about. When we were stooking I stood on the mouth of the nest and some furious wasps attacked me. I let out a yelp and Frank came running, pitchfork at the ready. One wasp was still sitting on my dungarees, trying to sting my leg. Frank held onto the dungarees and hit the wasp with the pitchfork handle, catching me a blow on my shin, and producing another yelp! I retreated to the far end of the field and left the men to do the stooking, with angry wasps buzzing round them. They didn't seem particularly worried but I hated wasps. In fact, during the wasp season each year there were times when I had to abandon my job, because of a persistent wasp. My other hatred was the small harvest bug: it had a nasty bite.

The most hilarious encounter with an insect was when I was milking Rose in the orchard one summer afternoon. She was tied to a fence post, to prevent her wandering off. It was a beautiful warm day and both of us were peacefully dreaming of other things, when a June bug, the big light-brown beetle with the most beautiful ruby eyes, landed on my knee. Not particularly alarming really, except that it chose to land where I had a hole in my jeans (John's old ones). I leapt off the milking stool, alarming Rose, who responded by putting her foot in the bucket and ruining the milk. I moved so quickly that the beetle did not have time to fly away and it disappeared from view. I soon discovered where it had gone! Down the hole in my jeans and it was on my leg. Oh! – such a panic! It was every bit as bad as getting into bed with a black beetle, which I once did. My mother was in the kitchen and had seen me leap to my feet. She called through the open window to ask what was wrong.

"A beetle," I replied, and undressed there and then. Luckily it was Sunday, Tom had gone home and there was no one else about. The beetle was found, looking a bit crumpled and, very bravely, I moved it out of the way using a handy twig. The milk was ruined and I had to filter it into a

Sue, a lovely Welsh cob.

calf's bucket, sterilise the pail again and return to finish the milking. Rose was a very understanding cow and took most things in her stride. She let down the remaining milk and the job was soon finished.

The V1s had been disrupting the south of England since May. Generally speaking we were outside their range. However, there were the few that managed to reach us. They were horribly low and spluttering as they came to the last drops of rocket fuel. One came over us on a Sunday. Again I was milking Rose in the orchard. She heard it first and turned her head, ears right forward to pick up the sound. A few seconds later I heard it too and stood up to see if I could locate it. There it was, very low and heading straight for us. It was close and I knew that if it cut out at that moment it would probably land on us, or at least very near us. I untied Rose from the post and wondered if I ought to fall flat, or run for the house. It was a moment of complete indecision and I remained rooted to the spot, watching the horrible thing. It was nearly overhead and almost scraping the tree tops when I realised that if it cut out it would drop in someone else's field and not on top of me. So I tied Rose up again and finished the milking, feeling an idiot for not seeking cover.

We knew all about V1s from my father, who had experienced them in London, but this was the first one we had seen. It fell harmlessly in a field and panicked a bunch of young steers. My father had been standing by the front door, watching the V1 approaching, and he had called to me to run to the house. When it was all over he asked me why I had stayed put. I told him I hadn't the faintest idea, and I still haven't. I can remember so clearly the sight of that V1 and the feeling of total disbelief as I watched it.

Then another one paid us a visit. It was a very misty morning, with visibility only a few yards. I was crossing the yard with buckets of water when I suddenly picked up the horrid roar of a V1. It was again very low and very close. This time I did not hesitate; I fell flat in the yard. There was no chance of seeing the rocket – the mist was too thick – but it definitely went overhead and cut out at once. It landed a great deal closer than the first one.

Jim was on his way through Sarratt when his horse, Dick, picked up the noise of the rocket. The mist was too thick for Jim to see it, but Dick reckoned it was coming straight for him, and the normally placid old horse became a bit jittery, until the rocket had passed overhead and was heading for us. There were others in the vicinity from time to time, but none as close as the first two.

It was late September and Rose had not been in season since calving. I decided I had better ask Mr Barr to examine her. I had hoped to have her served in August because a May calf suited me very well. Mr Barr gave Rose a thorough examination and said she was infertile, due to insufficient protein in her diet. The pound of cattle cake a day was totally insufficient for a milking cow and though she had never been hungry, she had not been well nourished. I felt shattered: my beautiful Rose would have no more calves. I would continue to milk her for six or seven months and then she would have to be slaughtered. It meant eventually buying another cow to replace her, because Jersey would not calve until early 1946. However, I need not worry about that for at least six months. The thought of losing Rose made me very sad: she would only be ten years old by the time she was slaughtered, which is no great age for a cow. We would all miss her: she was a great character.

The new grass, in the top half of the field, was ready for light grazing and Rose, accompanied by Jersey and Rosemary, was put there for a few hours each day. Rose couldn't believe her eyes and immediately she was through the gate, put her head down and began ripping up the young grass. She hardly moved from where she was. Rosemary did not eat very much but skipped round the field because it was somewhere new which had to be explored. Jersey followed Rose and filled herself with good grass. The controlled grazing did improve the grass and I decided that I would close the field in December and hope for hot weather in June 1945, so that we could cut the grass at its very best.

Harvesting being over, muckspreading, followed by ploughing, would be the next task. Then potato lifting, sprout picking and all the usual winter jobs. The seasons came and went at an alarming pace. I was so busy there hardly seemed time for anything else.

Threshing found us going round all the familiar farms. We began, as usual, with Percy Baldwin's corn, at Bulstrode Farm; then we moved to Will Bryant at Street Farm; followed by Ben Potter, Venus Hill Farm; and Alf Smith up Water Lane. The most interesting sight that year was watching Bill Harris easing the huge traction engine along the lane beside our orchard. He was on his way down to the fields Mr Martin owned, and behind the big Fowler was a fleet of machinery. It was towing the drum, the bailer, the chaff cutter, the trusser and the elevator. The ground was a veritable quagmire so the "spuds" were on the wheels, but not a full set, so each wheel slipped until it came to the next few spuds. I couldn't understand how it was that one wheel appeared to be doing the work while the

Rose of Stocks Hotel. Born in Guernsey.

other slipped. I never realised that by then all traction engines were fitted with a differential, so Bill eased the Fowler by using alternate wheels. Steamrollers were not fitted, so if it was necessary to turn a sharp corner a pin was put through one back wheel, to immobilise it, while the other wheel did the work.

For a long time I did not understand how a huge traction engine could be modestly rated at 7 NHP (Nominal Horse Power). Surely it couldn't be the equivalent of just seven horses? I finally discovered that during the last century it had been a way of deceiving the Government and county councils, because of the terrific opposition to steam engines being on the roads. The NHP was a fraction of the actual horsepower, but it sounded somewhat less formidable to have an engine of 7 NHP rather than 56 NHP! Multiplying the NHP by eight gave you the actual horsepower.

When we were threshing it was always Jim's task to look after the sacks. As soon as one was full he would unclip it and move it to one side. Another member of the team would be ready to clip the next sack in place, so as not to waste any corn. The sacks were big and weighed two hundredweight, and Jim, along with a few others, could carry them easily. When we had finished threshing and were preparing to leave the site, Frank would go round making sure nothing dangerous to animals or children had been left behind. Two of the things we always had to look out for were odd bits of binder twine from the trusser and wire from the baler. The wire could only too easily get wound round the axle of a vehicle and the twine could be eaten by cows and calves.

Christmas was here again and we had our usual fare of either a home-grown cockerel, a local goose or a couple of ducks, bought from Mrs Pritchard. We couldn't spare any of ours and for some reason we never raised any ducklings. In those days Christmas was not the extended holiday it is now. I had two days off and then it was back to work.

The Christmas tree caused a great deal of fun each year. In 1940 Phillips had noticed three small Christmas trees growing on a bit of land between us and Mrs Martin's. We were not sure who owned them so when Phillips suggested we dig up the largest for Christmas, we all went out to take stock of the situation. The trees were close together and we decided no one would notice if one was borrowed. We potted it in a large bucket of earth, watered it well and took it indoors. After twelfth night it was replanted on a good dollop of manure and left in peace. It survived, so we did the same in 1941. The tree had grown a bit but it still fitted in the house. Out it went once more and to our amazement seemed none the worse for wear, probably because we had no central heating. We used it for about six years before it became too tall for the low ceilings. Once we failed to remove some tinsel, and it escaped our notice when we took the tree out. The next day Phillips happened to notice it when he arrived in the morning, so he quickly removed it.

During the winter months Sue never did any work for Frank, so in November her shoes were removed, her hooves trimmed and she went unshod until about March. Any jobs she did for us were only around the smallholding, which did not damage her feet. Frank's horses were shod for winter work on the slippery roads, which meant fitting "roughs". The shoes were made as usual but each had two holes, about three-eighths of an inch in diameter, drilled on either side, into which the roughs could be screwed when there was snow and ice on the roads. It prevented a horse slipping and perhaps breaking a leg. The roughs were small spikes which measured about an inch in length – enough to grip the snow, or stick into ice.

The marrow-stem kale had exceeded all my expectations. Some of it was nearly six feet tall and had huge leaves and very thick stems. Rose was delighted and munched her way through a whole plant at a time. The stems had to be split to make it easier for her to eat them and all she left was the very tough end and the root. We had plenty of root crops and greens for the animals that winter, but we did have to buy extra hay.

By now the war in Europe appeared to be drawing to a close and blackout restrictions were lifted. That meant we could at last have a really big bonfire. Jim had done some more pruning and general tidying up for us and we had amassed a considerable amount of wood during the years. Some of it we had been able to use on the slow-burning stove we had in the lounge, but the rest had been stocked at the back of the pond, where the hemlock had grown. Jim arrived early one morning and started the bonfire. By four thirty he began damping it down so that it could be left all night unattended. He did so by drawing the ash carefully up the sides of the fire, which still stood about two and a half feet high. The fire was solid, and had burnt with an intense heat. When it was completely covered with ash Jim went home, saying he would be back next day to burn the rest of the wood. I looked out of the window several times during the evening but there wasn't even a glimmer. Next morning all Jim had to do was carefully stroke down some of the ash, gently stir the fire, and it sprang back into life. It really was amazing.

It was time to think about a replacement cow for Rose. She would be dry by March so I needed to buy a milking cow, which I would keep until Jersey calved. I decided to phone Mr Fitch: he might have an in-calf Guernsey cow to sell. Also I wanted to find out if he was still interested in buying Rosemary. Mr Fitch came to look at Rosemary and he liked her so much that be bought her there and then. She was nine months old and the very image of her mother, except for her pale skin. In return he sold me a very attractive pedigree Guernsey heifer, due to calve in March. We named her Clover, after an Alderney cow my maternal grandmother used to tell me about. Alderneys are similar to Guernseys.

Grannie Laura was Devonshire born but had lived most of her life in Birkenhead. When she was a little girl she used to spend the summer on her grandparents' farm near Bideford. She could remember the big dairy in which they made cheeses, beautiful Devonshire clotted cream, butter, and curd cheese. The dairy maids skimmed the cream with their hands, and evidently the thickness of the cream was mainly due to Clover. Grannie remembered how the local children would often arrive at the back door, sent by their mothers, to ask if Mrs Borough could spare a drop of milk. The jugs they carried held at least a quart, and they always returned home with them filled to the brim. But, regretfully, our Clover would not emulate her namesake. Her skin was pale and her cream would not be yellow like Rose's.

Rose was only producing about two pints a day. Sadly I decided the time had come to get rid of her; I couldn't put it off any longer. Clover was due to calve in about a fortnight. I had a word with Frank and he gave me the name of a man who would come and collect Rose and slaughter her. I phoned him and the next afternoon he arrived with a large cattle truck. I fetched Rose from the field and led her out to the waiting lorry. The man took her halter off and handed it to me.

"You go back inside," he said in a kindly way, "and leave all this to me. I'm going to slaughter her here, and then load her into the lorry." I shot back into the house and waited until the lorry drove away. Poor Rose; I doubted if we would have another cow like her. She had been with us for a little under four years. She had adapted to her new way of life without any fuss. She became used to finding cats curled up in the hay in her manger. I don't think they ever got used to being woken up by a cow breathing heavily on them! One day she found a hen laying an egg in the trough in the brick cowshed. She ate the egg before I could get to it. The hen nearly had hysterics. When we put Rose on one of the lawns to do a bit of trimming for us, she stuck her head in through the dining room window and pruned Mum's succulent. It never really recovered. One of the old apple trees in the orchard was small and occasionally produced a few very sweet apples. One year Rose discovered how tasty they were and stood under the tree with her head up in the branches, which she shook vigorously until apples dropped down. I will always remember shouting at her from the drive, and the way she stuck her head out of the branches as though to say, "What's the matter now?" Nothing really bothered her, not even the bats which suddenly took up residence in the open barn and would flit round her when I was doing the evening milking. They flew between her horns, and all round her legs, after minute insects. She never moved, but when the same thing happened to Jersey all hell was let loose. While the bats were about I had to milk Jersey in the brick shed.

Chapter Seven

March 1945 began with Clover having her calf. I brought her into the big barn and made up a deep bed of straw for her. She seemed very uneasy and I wondered if anything was wrong. Mrs Martin came and looked at her and advised waiting a bit longer. Heifers, she assured me, were sometimes very slow to calve. By teatime the calf's front hooves were showing and Clover was even more uneasy, so I fetched Frank and Jim. Jim examined the unhappy animal to make sure the calf's head was not bent back. Everything was in place but it was a big calf with a big head, Jim said. It was going to be another bull. We seemed destined to have a preponderance of bull calves! Mrs Martin had a calving rope and I dashed off to borrow it.

Jim tied the rope round the calf's feet and he and Frank stood ready to pull when Clover strained. I was at the head end trying to comfort a distraught animal. The bull did not want to be born and it was quite a while before Frank and Jim managed to pull it out. Once it was all over Clover seemed none the worse for wear and she was up, licking her calf and mooing gently to it.

Two days later she had milk fever. This came as a great surprise because I had read it was most unusual in a first calver, and more so in one that had had a prolonged and difficult calving. It was when I called Clover in for the afternoon milking that I noticed something was badly wrong. She was standing outside the back door of the barn and staggered a bit as she turned round to walk in. She then collided with the door as though she was blind, and all the alarm bells started ringing in my head. I guided her into her pen and dashed off to phone for the vet. By now Mr Barr had retired and we had changed to Mr Dixon from Berkhamsted. He was out, but his assistant Wendy Shollick came dashing up and Clover had an injection of calcium boro-gluconate in the shoulder, and one for luck into a vein. Within a remarkably short time she was up and better and able to eat a big meal. For several days I was careful not to milk her right out after her calf had had its fill. At the end of the first week she was perfectly fit and her milk yield had began to climb, so I bought two more

*Pa's four ducks. Side gate where Cosmo and Neda met in
a head-on collision.*

calves, both shorthorns. Clover was a heavier milker than Rose had ever
been and gave at least four gallons a day for quite a while, but the butterfat content was lower and the cream was pale to match her pale skin. We
had been spoilt by Rose!

Clover was a quiet, obedient cow. She never tried to break out, she
always did as she was told, she was easy to handle and easy to milk, and
after all these years I can hardly remember her!

Peter and I had become engaged in February and one Monday, early
in April, I received a letter from him saying he would be home on leave in
July. I wrote back immediately to say, "Let's get married." That evening
I decided to study the marriage service and inadvisably expressed my
objections to some of it in no uncertain terms. The Almighty was not
pleased and decided that punishment was necessary. The method He chose
was to cause me embarrassment and acute anxiety.

The next day, Tuesday, was "pie and sausage day" and Frank
used to let me have a little time off so I could dash down to the village
and buy some "Woolton" pies and doubtful sausages. (We did wonder what was in some of them!) It was a beautiful day and I was feeling supremely happy as I rushed home from the farm to collect my bicycle, some money and the shopping list. The bicycle had developed a flat
tyre and the pump was missing. I dashed into the house and hunted high
and low, finally finding it in the dresser drawer. I pumped up the tyre

and made my way to the back gates. Only when I was through them both did I remember the ration books. By now Rufus knew that I was going out, and I had wasted a valuable ten minutes. I hated being late back at the farm. Rufus followed me to the gate and let out a doleful yowl as I peddled frantically up the lane. Like a fool I had trusted to luck that no yard gates were open – I certainly didn't remember noticing that any of them were. I soon forgot all about Rufus in my determination to get the shopping done quickly.

I had just reached Frenches Farm, where Miss Hawes lived, when I heard remarkably heavy breathing behind me. I looked back and there, to my horror, was Rufus running along the grass bank. I hadn't the time to turn round and take him back, and anyhow he enjoyed being out so much that I doubted if he would follow me. I obviously had no lead with me, so I decided to pedal faster and hope to lose him for a bit. He kept up with me with such ease that I began to get bothered. It looked as though I was not going to lose him at all.

Luckily his road sense was good: he kept out of the way of all cars and always looked before crossing a road, so I began to feel a bit more cheerful. Perhaps he would behave well after all. He had been out with me on several occasions but always on a lead and walking to heel.

I went to Simmonds Nurseries first for some seeds. The hill up from the crossroads is a long drag on a bicycle and here Rufus overtook me. He found an open gate and popped inside. There was a very old man bending over some plants. Rufus went up to him and sniffed his hand. The old man yelled and Rufus bounded out and went on up the road. I looked the other way and pretended the dog was nothing to do with me. The old man said nothing.

I reached the nurseries and turned up the short drive. Rufus followed. I had a few awkward moments convincing him that he was to sit on the step and not follow me into the shop. I asked for the seeds. Through the window I noticed that Rufus had moved and was examining some ornamental shrubs. I feared that any minute now he would lift a leg and ruin them. I dashed out and got him back and sat him down again. I had just paid for the seeds when a small girl, carrying a basket, came along the drive. She stopped and looked at Rufus. He looked at her and then with a growl he leaped up and chased her out into the road. The child screamed and I dashed after Rufus and brought him back. Mrs Simmonds look at me coldly.

"Too big a dog to have running loose," she said sternly. I agreed and explained what had happened. Rufus chose that moment to walk over a flower bed, so I left quickly.

I decided I would disown the dog. I wouldn't speak to him or recognise him. As he was ahead of me now it was fairly easy to look uncon-
cerned – far easier than when he was following me only a foot or two
from my back wheel! I decided to give the butchers a miss; I wanted to get
home as quickly as possible and would try for the pies at the grocers. We
set off down the hill, Rufus still ahead. On the left-hand side of the road
there was a small low pram, the mother standing with her back to it as she
chatted to another woman. They neither of them saw Rufus as he trotted
up, but the mother turned just in time to see Rufus' large head disappear
under the hood. I wasn't near enough to see but I am sure he licked the
baby's face. The mother shouted and Rufus was off, bounding down the
hill. As I passed the pram I was having terrible trouble with the chain of
my bicycle. I hadn't the courage to look at either woman.

Rufus had disappeared and when I reached the crossroads there was
still no sign of him. I got off my bicycle and stood outside the grocers,
trying to pluck up courage to leave him, wherever he was and whatever
he might be doing. Suddenly I saw him, at the top of the hill by the post
office, as he came out of somebody's gateway. At the same moment an old
man on a bike came over the brow of the hill. I was so relieved to see Rufus
again, much as I wanted to lose him, that I did a very foolish thing: I whistled. He turned and began trotting down the hill, following the old man.
The trot turned into a canter as the hill got the better of him and he was
right in line with the bicycle. At this point the old man must have heard the
same heavy breathing that I had heard, and he half turned his head. He did
not dare to look right round because he was going quite quickly for one as
old as he. The glance must have been enough and a look of horror crossed
his face. Rufus was quite out of control: all legs and paws and a huge
floppy tongue. There was nothing I could do but reverently hope that one
or other of them would change course. Rufus suddenly got out of step as
the hill levelled out and that slowed him down enough to enable the poor
old man to pull well ahead of him. He was so shaken that he never stopped
at the crossroads, but cycled on.

Rufus came to a stop beside me. He was totally out of breath but
quite happy. I decided to go to the post office first and Rufus followed
me up the hill, back the way he had just come. It was a steep hill and
I had to wheel my bicycle, with Rufus walking behind me. Thankfully
I reached the post office without incident. I leant my bicycle against the pillar box and left Rufus sitting by the telephone kiosk. There was a queue of

three people ahead of me in the post office, so I had to wait several minutes. When two of the customers had gone I popped my head outside to make sure Rufus was all right. He had disappeared. I stood on the step and whistled. Nothing happened except a terse reminder from the postmaster that dogs were NOT allowed in the post office. I was feeling rather cross by now and explained that he was too big to fit in the post office anyhow, but that I did not wish him to go too far. Rufus did not appear so I went back inside to buy some stamps.

When I finally got outside there was a woman standing by the pillar box with a long strip of twopenny-ha'penny stamps. She was holding them in one hand and some letters in the other. Rufus appeared, trotting along the road from the direction of the common. He saw me and came straight to where I was standing with my bicycle. The woman was surprised to see such a large dog, and very nervously said, "Good doggie", which of course made Rufus turn to her. He put his head up to the hand holding the stamps and the whole strip lay along his nose, nearly to his eyes. If he had given one lick…! I pulled Rufus away by his collar and set off down the hill, back to the grocers. I kept both brakes on and went down very slowly and Rufus trotted along in a small ditch.

As it was a warm day, the shop door was propped open and Rufus shot straight inside and got behind the counter before he was seen. I bun-

Tenements Farm from the field. It shows the extension built in 1932.

dled him out. On his second attempt he nearly got into the small office at the back of the shop. The third time he came in there were many more people in the shop and someone pushed him out. He gave up and lay down in the sun and waited for me.

A few minutes later Mrs Whitlock, who lived near us, came into the shop. She laughed when she saw me and said, "Rufus is chasing that brown dog all the way home." I grabbed the sausages and pies and rushed out, jumped on my bicycle and headed for home. Sure enough there was Rufus about a quarter of a mile ahead, going up the incline towards our lane. The brown dog shot into its own garden and Rufus slowed down to a walk. I called to him and he waited until I reached him and then trotted on.

Sitting on the grass bank opposite The Boot public house was Frank's three-year-old grandson, David. The young boy's mother, Mary, was talking to another woman and a black Labrador dog was standing nearby. Rufus trotted straight up to David and licked his face. The child pushed him away and the Labrador, after one look at Rufus, turned and ran up the road, with Rufus after it. He still seemed to have plenty of energy and the last I saw of the two dogs was a cloud of dust as they floundered over a heap of rubbish further up the road. I felt quite tired when I reached home. It had been an exhausting shopping expedition and I vowed I would never again criticise the marriage service. I saw Rufus as I was leaving the house after lunch. He was coming up the orchard, looking very tired.

About the middle of April I decided it was time to find a suitable bull for Jersey. She was eighteen months old and had grown into a very pretty heifer. Mrs Martin suggested we should put her to the young Ayrshire bull which was running with about a dozen cows in the field across the lane. The bull was very young – about two years old – and he had been with the cows for about four weeks. They were all true matrons: there wasn't a young one amongst them and, though they were definitely coming into season, not one of them would permit the young bull to serve them. I had watched him approaching one of the cows in a most apprehensive manner, but as soon as he was near enough to mount, she swung round and rammed him with her horns. Defeated, he retreated. The next day he tried another one, with the same result, and I felt very sorry for him. He spent most of each day forlornly grazing by himself. I felt sure it could not be good for his health, so when Mrs Martin suggested using him on Jersey, I immediately agreed.

Mrs Martin brought him into our field and introduced him to Jersey, who had been in season for about half a day. They rubbed noses and Jersey obviously thought he was a nice young bull. I think he was decidedly relieved to find a cow that did not ram him with her horns, and Jersey was successfully mated. A few days later I noticed the young bull had been removed from those old matrons and the old bull replaced him. There was no further trouble from the cows.

Clover and Jersey got on well together. Jersey was not afraid of her and Clover, who was a mild cow, did not bully her as Rose had done. It was about now that Jersey damaged one of her horns and spoilt her good looks. At milking time I had started tying Jersey up in one of the standings in the brick cowshed, to get her used to the routine. I also massaged her udder for a moment or two each time, in the hopes it would make her an easy cow to milk right from the start.

While waiting for her food to be put into the trough the silly animal would toss her head about and one day she crashed her horn against the brick partition, and broke it. Blood poured down her face and she shook her head, splattering it everywhere. I rushed indoors and got all the ice out of the refrigerator and made an ice pack out of an old towel and rushed back to Jersey. She was standing still with the blood still dripping a bit as it started to clot. I patted her and tried to get the ice pack on to her horn. It was obviously very tender and she backed away to the full length of the tether. There she was stuck and very gently I packed the ice round her horn and kept it there for a good ten minutes. It melted and water ran down her face, which she didn't like, but a least the bleeding had stopped and I hoped perhaps any pain she had felt. She had learnt her lesson and never again did she throw her head about.

Secretly I was rather pleased it had happened, because her habit of tossing her head about had cost me a black eye when she caught me an awful blow on my left eyebrow. Eventually the horn, which was nowhere near fully grown, came loose and dropped off, leaving a new and small one in its place. I kept the old one for years and finally lost it during a house move.

It was time to prepare Sue for her return to work. During the winter I never groomed her and she grew a good coat, which by springtime was thick and matted and she looked very untidy. She was beginning to shed it and a considerable amount of grooming would be needed to make her look a tidy horse once more. Any time now Frank might want her for some of the little jobs that always seemed to crop up in the spring. A bit of horse manure for someone's garden; a sack or two of potatoes to someone who had run out; trusses of hay for a horse, or bales of straw for its bedding. My float was just the right size for many of those jobs and a bit of work would do Sue a lot of good: she had had a lazy winter. I particularly wanted her to look clean, so she was brushed every day and wiped down with a leather, until her old coat had gone and a nice shiny horse was back again. She had also had her shoes put back on and I used to paint her hooves with Neat's foot oil to make them shine. She had a very thick wiry mane with which I could do nothing. It was always bushy so one day I cut it all off, except for the forelock. I wasn't really in favour of doing such a thing but the improvement was so great that I was quite happy. She looked elegant and was ready for any work that Frank wanted her to do.

I remember grooming Rose one year when she was shedding her winter coat. I had gone into the top half of the field, where she was grazing, and started to brush her. She stopped eating and stood, as though mesmerised, with her eyes half closed. I gave her a good brushing, finishing with her face, paying particular attention to the hair across her forehead and behind her horns because she had bits of straw stuck there. She enjoyed tossing straw about, if she had the chance. Having finished, I turned away and walked back to the gate. Rose let out a disgusted "moo" and was after me, waving her horns in a menacing manner. I had to brush her face and forehead again, and then I ran quickly for the gate. I just beat her to it. After that I only brushed her when she was tied up after the evening milking.

Peter Hanscomb, back row, third from the left. In 1939.

Jersey hated being brushed. She had a much finer coat than Rose and, I suppose, a more sensitive skin. So I only wiped her down occasionally with a leather. She always looked silky and never had a thick winter coat.

The next momentous occasion was VE Day on May the 10th. We had decided we would celebrate with a bonfire and fireworks. Alan Brock was a friend of Pa's and he sent us a magnificent selection of fireworks, ready for the great day. We collected all the brushwood we could – we hadn't much else to burn since Jim's enormous bonfire, and stacked it ready in the orchard, on what was to have been a tennis court, only the war had intervened and spoilt that project. It had been turfed in the spring of 1939 and was the one bit of decent grass in the whole of the orchard when the sheep arrived.

We let off the fireworks after supper on the evening of May the 10th, having shut the dogs in the house, tied up the cows in the brick shed, shut the calves in the barn and moved Sue to the top half of the field. Only the cats were out and about and they all congregated in the open barn in the manger. You would have thought we had had enough of thumps and bangs, but we were like children! Thunderflashes were going off left, right and centre; the roman candles in those far off days were far more spectacular than anything now; and the golden rain was a huge shower that lit up the drive and we thought was going to set fire to Tom. He was having the time of his life and had put himself in charge of the fireworks. His wife Elsie, watching him, said, "He's just like a small boy." We threw jumping jacks into the bonfire and rushed round waving at one another all the fireworks labelled: "MAY BE HELD IN THE HAND".

It was a wonderful party and next morning we had to spend quite a while removing all the debris from the drive. The war in Europe was over, but work would continue as usual for a long time.

One of the first jobs was to rewire the barns. We had had electric lights in both of them before the war but the bulbs had been removed and the switches taped up. It was marvellous to have the lights back again. All through the war we had used a large hurricane lamp with the glass painted blue. It did give just enough light to prevent us from injuring ourselves when we had to go into the barns after dark. Mum always tried to be finished by dark, which was about 5.30 pm, as we were on summer time from October to March and the dreaded double summer time for the rest of the year. Occasionally I reached home at about 4.30 pm and if there wasn't much to do I sometimes managed to finish before dark. We always made our final rounds at about 10 pm to make sure all the animals were safe for the night.

It was shortly after VE Day that I suddenly decided I would try and breed from Sue. Frank warned me that horses were nothing like as fertile as cattle and at eight years old Sue might prove difficult to get in foal. Still there was no harm in trying and luckily there was a beautiful Welsh Cob stallion about two miles away. Mares, like cows, come in season every three weeks and remain on heat for about a week. The trouble is that it is nearly impossible to detect that they are in season.

The best arrangement would be for Sue to run with the stallion for at least a month. Longer would have been better, but she would have to be back for haymaking by the end of June. I rode over one Saturday to see the stallion and his owner and we agreed that Sue should be with them for the last week of May and the first three weeks in June, providing she could be spared. I had a word with Frank to make sure it would not upset his arrangements and he was quite happy for Sue to spend four weeks with the stallion.

Full of hope, I took Sue to meet the stallion towards the end of May. Fortunately she came on heat – at least I thought she did – a few days before, which was most convenient. I rode her over and Pa followed, some twenty minutes later, to collect me. I dismounted by the gate and Sue noticed the stallion at the bottom of the field. She let out an ear-splitting neigh and he came galloping up to greet her. I managed to get the saddle and bridle off, but it was a struggle. She simply would not stand still and was trying to rub noses with the stallion. I left her head collar on, having been warned that she would probably be difficult to catch in a month's time, and after struggling to open the gate with the stallion leaning over it to get at Sue, the two animals finally met.

Judging by the interest the stallion was showing, Sue was undoubtedly on heat. They squealed at one another and raced down the field, bucking and kicking with delight. Pa and I watched them for a few minutes and then drove home.

While Sue was away Clover was served by the old Ayrshire bull. As Mr Fitch had offered to buy her back when we no longer needed her, I had felt it was a bit unfair to land him with a crossbred calf. He wasn't worried and said he would have no difficulty in finding a buyer for the calf if it was a heifer, and if it was a bull it would go to market.

The month passed quickly and it was time to collect Sue. Frank warned me not to try riding her back.

"She'll be skittish and will probably shy at anything," he said.

I took his advice as Pa dropped me at the field and left me to catch my horse. I had plenty of snacks in my pockets and a rope to thread though the buckle under her chin. But first, attract the attention of your horse! I called her. She looked up as much as to say "I think I know that voice" then returned to the business of grazing. I walked slowly down the field, calling her name. It wasn't Sue who responded, but the stallion. He came up to me and sniffed my pockets to see if I had any goodies. I shooed him away but he came back. I swear I could have caught him a dozen times but Sue just kept at arm's length. There was only one thing for it: feed a snack to the stallion and walk towards the gate. He would follow and with luck, so would Sue. The ruse worked and I reached the gate with the two horses. The stallion had been munching bits of toast and pieces of potato as he followed me and now I offered a bit to Sue. She knew I wanted to catch her and was most reluctant to take any food, so I gave it to the stallion and then held out another bit for Sue. Finally, she could resist no longer and came just close enough for me to grab her. She let out a neigh and pulled away from me. I clung on for dear life while I threaded the rope through the buckle, knotted it tightly and moved to open the gate. The stallion was in the way, with his back to me. I didn't like being behind him – he might kick – so I threw the last bit of potato ahead of him. Luckily he saw it fall and moved off to eat it. Sue and I were through that gate in a flash. I had just closed it when the stallion finished the bit of potato and came back for more.

Sue let out a high-pitched neigh as I began leading her away, and the stallion followed her on the other side of the hedge. Progress was very slow. The two horses had a lot to say to one another and Sue would not walk any faster than the stallion. When we reached the boundary of the field Sue stopped and I had to give her a sharp flick with the other end of the rope to make her move on. The stallion began neighing and running to and fro as we disappeared from sight. Long after we had left him he was neighing to Sue, who was deafening me each time she replied. At last they could no longer hear one another and I then realised what Frank meant.

With no stallion to distract her Sue began taking an interest in where we were. The world immediately became a dangerous place, and she shied at every car. Then she wanted to trot. She eyed all dogs suspiciously and finally tried to turn round and go back. It was very much like having a small version of young Kitty to deal with, but luckily she was much smaller so I could just control her. We finally reached home and, without thinking, I did a stupid thing. I put her in the field with Clover and Jersey.

Sue went barmy and dashed round the field in full gallop. Clover and Jersey saw her coming and took off in the opposite direction. When Sue began a second lap of the field I just managed to get the two cows out and shut the gate before Sue reached them. She spent quite some time trotting up and down, neighing and snorting, before she finally quietened down. There was probably about a fortnight to go before she would be hay raking, if the weather held, and I trusted that by then she would have forgotten her holiday with the stallion.

We did manage to do some haymaking before Peter arrived in England from Brussels, and then the weather, which had been unsettled, broke with an awful thunderstorm which delayed his crossing the channel and he only just reached Chipperfield in time. We were married on the 17th July and had a week's honeymoon down in Devon. It was the first holiday I had taken since September 1940, when I was sent to the seaside by our doctor. I was suffering from the most awful attack of sinusitis I had ever had and luckily the sea air cured it completely.

Peter and I were very lucky: the monumental thunderstorm seemed to have cleared the air and we had a week of hot sunny weather. It was very strange not to have to rush out and do the milking or feed the calves, and to begin with I felt guilty at having such a lazy time. Luckily Mrs Martin very kindly did the morning milking and Tom did the evening. The calves were easy to feed as they were still having milk from the calf feeder, and Jersey was not having any extra food so there was nothing to do for her except make sure she had plenty of water. Frank didn't borrow Sue while I was away, so she had a lazy week. The time passed far too quickly and before we knew where we were, Peter had returned to Brussels and I was back on the hayrake.

There was a bit of a diversion during haymaking when I had to help out at Woodmans Farm. They were using their Fordson tractor-towing trailers fitted with upright laddering at each end, and we could pack quite a big load onto one trailer. I was invited by the driver, Colin, to have a go, without the trailer of course. I couldn't change gear at all, though steering it was easy enough. I remember one old farmer saying they weren't much use: drank gallons of paraffin and there was no useful pile of manure next morning!

Every three weeks I was examining Sue to see if she was coming into season but there was no indication at all. I began to feel hopeful but Frank warned me not to be too optimistic because of the difficulty of knowing when a mare was on heat. If she was in foal it would be born the following April, so she would stop work in November, which would be quite convenient.

It was now the middle of August and harvesting was in full swing. One evening I decided to ride home on Dick. The cart was being left in the field

Married in 1945.

ready for the next day, so to save walking I climbed up onto the old horse. I sat behind the cart saddle he was wearing and never took into account the buckle from which the first of two straps went down to the breeching strap. I realised there was something hard just pressing a little on the tail end of my spine, but I didn't think any harm would come from it. When I slid off Dick in the farmyard my tail felt distinctly sore and as I walked home it chafed and felt much worse. Mum examined it for me and roared with laughter. I had skinned myself! It was extremely painful when I had my bath and had to be smothered with ointment. Luckily the next day was Saturday and I only did the essential jobs. By Monday it was very much better and I didn't try riding behind the cart saddle again.

Mum discovered, to her dismay, that I had used molasses for cooking. I had run out of black treacle. We couldn't buy it very often and I did like parkin cake. I had taken some molasses, heated it, strained it and used it in the cake. The result was excellent – better than with black treacle – and for a while Mum suspected nothing! It was Pa who announced that the parkin seemed richer in flavour than usual.

"Made with molasses?" he asked. I looked at Mum.

"You haven't been cooking with molasses, have you?" she asked.

I hesitated a moment. "Yes," I replied, "but no one is likely to ask me."

"You were not going to tell me, were you?" queried Mum.

"No," I replied truthfully. I had kept quiet because I knew quite well that, if ever we were asked if we used molasses, I would be able to say "no" whereas Mum would have had the greatest difficulty. I told her I had not let on, to protect her! I got a very old-fashioned look. We had a bit of molasses left over because we had decided not to make any more silage. Without Phillips it would have been a much harder job.

Arriving at the farm one Monday in September I was mightily surprised to see two little donkeys peering through the gate the far side of the yard. What on earth was Frank doing with donkeys? It transpired that their owner had died and Frank had been asked to find a suitable home for them. They were a Jack and a Jenny, brother and sister, about six years old, who had never been separated. Frank had been asked to find a buyer who would take both of them. Finally, he found someone in Bovingdon who wanted a donkey for his children and had managed to persuade him to take both of them. I was asked to deliver them.

"Most donkeys have to be driven; they cannot be led," said Frank. "If you get in front of them they will stop dead."

The donkeys had halters on with very long ropes and I set off with the pair walking in front of me. Frank had given me a long stick with which to guide the offside donkey, should he wander towards the middle of the road. They were pretty animals: an attractive oatmeal colour with the mark of the cross, in dark brown, on the withers. Frank pointed it out to me. I had never noticed it before.

The little animals were very easy to control and a tap with the stick kept them in line and on the move. When we were about halfway there I decided to try leading them. They were so obedient I couldn't believe they wouldn't follow me. So I shortened the halter ropes and slowly moved up towards their heads. The minute I drew level with them they stopped dead. I stood in front and tugged at their halters. They seemed to dig their tiny hooves into the road as they leaned backwards, stubbornness written all over their faces. So I returned to my original position and off they went. I tried it again, but the same thing happened. Frank was quite right.

By November I reluctantly came to the conclusion that Sue was not in foal. She was still as slim as ever. I was bitterly disappointed: I had wanted to try bringing up a foal. I was full of harebrained ideas and wanted to see if it would be possible to break in a young horse. I briefly wondered if it would be worth putting Sue to the stallion again in 1946, but decided against it. She would have her foal in 1947 and by then Peter and I might have our own baby. It was better to forget all about it, but it was a big disappointment.

Thirty-six years later we went to the Ploughing Championships near Wing in Buckinghamshire. While the others took a look at the tractors, some in difficulties because of the wet ground, I went and drooled over the horses. One pair: two mares, looked odd. They were working quite well though both had a slightly tight-lipped look. But there was more it to it than that: they both worked with their ears nearly flat on their heads, which gave them a bad-tempered look. Yet they were not showing any signs of being cross. For quite a while I watched them from a distance, until it suddenly dawned on me that they had no blinkers on their bridles. That must be why they looked different.

I still wasn't satisfied so I walked down beside the rope barrier to be opposite them when they came up the field. Intrigued, I waited as they hauled the plough towards me. There was still something that puzzled me. The ploughman stopped and the horses' noses were within patting distance of the rope barrier. A child stood on tiptoe and stroked one of the mares on the nose. The horse was standing there, impassive, ears now upright but turned all the while as though waiting for some noise from behind. She was a roan, probably about ten years old, patient-looking; and her partner was about the same age but dark brown. They were both standing quite still. No fidgeting with their feet, no fretting with the bit, no dribbling, no pulling on the plough lines. Then I suddenly realised they were bitless. They were wearing head collars only and the plough lines were attached to the outside buckles at the side of their nosebands. No wonder those horses looked so different. They were working to spoken commands, hence the turned ears. The corners of their mouths were soft. They weren't tight-lipped, as I thought; they simply had no bits to worry them and no cause to keep opening their mouths. They were possibly a bit slower than the other teams but it was quite fascinating to watch them obey the ploughman's every command. So it was possible to break a horse for work without the use of a bit. My question had a last been answered!

By November 1945 I had sold the last two heifer calves. Clover was due to calve at the end of March 1946 and her milk production had taken a dive in the past month. Still, I couldn't complain: she had been a very good milker. Jersey was due to calve at the beginning of February and I planned to have Clover dry by the middle of January. Mr Fitch would then buy her back and once more Frank offered to come to the rescue and let me have some milk to tide us over.

I wasn't sorry to see the back of the two calves. Rufus had discovered how to open the big gate which led from our field into the lane. It was a double gate made of metal and chain-link fencing, with a bar which went into a plate in the ground, and a sliding latch. Rufus discovered that all he had to do was lift the bar out of the ground, then throw his body against the gate, push hard once or twice, and it would open. He did it several times before we found a way of stopping him and on more than one occasion out went the calves. They were shorthorns of a remarkably lively disposition. It was quite revealing to observe the totally different temperaments of all the calves I had reared. There were no two alike: some were lively, some were quiet, some were bold and some were timid; but the two shorthorns I had that year were the most troublesome.

On the final occasion that the two were let out, I was at home by myself. It was a Saturday. Mum and Pa had gone shopping, and Tom hadn't yet arrived. I happened to look out of a bedroom window as I did the rounds of dusting and mopping, just in time to see two calves skip out of the field and down the lane. I rushed downstairs and fled to the gate in the wall. With luck I would just be in time to stop the calves going any further down the lane. Slowly I opened the gate, so as not to frighten them, and peered out. They were standing about twelve feet away, eating the grass on the verge. I managed to get behind them and got them to walk quietly or they would skip away from me. But there was one big problem: it needed two people because somehow I had to make them turn to the right to get them back through the field gate. If they continued in a straight line; the next stop would be the road, and I didn't fancy my chances if they got that far. I stood still for a moment and in despair I thought, "Please, God, stop those calves." They took several more steps and then suddenly stopped. Both were looking at something in the lane. I moved very slowly forward because I was sure they were about to run, and I wanted to be sure they went into the field. The next instant they turned and bolted back to the field. I moved quickly behind them and shut the gates. Once they were inside they felt safe and both turned to look at the spot where something had stood. There was no doubt about it.

Peter suddenly had three days leave towards the end of November and we began making plans for when he was demobilised, which he reckoned would be April 1946. My Aunt and Uncle had been sent to India by Lever Brothers and the cottage was empty. Mum and Pa suggested we should move in there until Peter got a job, so it was agreed we would take it over in April.

Threshing time was round once more and this would be my last winter with that magnificent Fowler traction engine. Though Didi and Bill were now quite used to having a girl working with them they still wouldn't tell me anything about how a steam engine worked. All they would say was "You won't understand" or "Girls aren't interested in steam engines". When I asked if I could stand on the footplate, to get a better look at the working parts, Bill refused to let me, on the grounds that it was dirty and I would probably burn myself. There was nothing I could do except hope that one day all would be revealed.

Chapter Eight

All the usual winter jobs were with us once more and, besides the sprout picking, there was another which I disliked intensely. During the winter months our outside tap always froze. Sometimes it could be cleared by pouring a kettle of boiling water over it, but if the frost had been severe the pipe would freeze in the wall where it went into the outside lavatory. There it joined the pipe that fed the cistern. We lagged it as best we could but to no avail. When the tap was frozen all the water for the animals had to be taken from the cold tap in the smaller of the two kitchen sinks. I used a watering can and a large bucket, and the job of filling all the water containers took ages. The mess I made on the tiled floor was similar to a minor flood. However careful I was, the spout of the can always cunningly wrapped itself round the leg of the kitchen table as I passed, causing a spill. The bucket banged itself against the sink on being lifted out, spilling more water. I had to fill at least five big containers to last the animals until I returned in the early evening. We had bought large round corrugated bins, which were about a third of a dustbin in height. The sheep had one of them. Rose had a large galvanised iron bath, because I soon found out that she liked to tip the smaller ones over when the water was low enough. The calves, when old enough to be outside, had one similar to the sheep and there was a spare, which was used in the pub's field. In the summer the hose would just reach across the drive to the top of the orchard, and to the gate into the field by Meadow View, so at least two or three bins could be filled quickly. The bucket and watering can were still needed for the remainder, but at least the outside tap could be used. The other problem was the speed with which the water sometimes froze, and on those days I had to go the rounds at lunchtime as well, breaking the ice and adding some boiling water to give them all a chance to have a drink before it froze again. In the severe cold all the animals, except the sheep, would be in for the night so buckets of water had to be offered to them last thing. I had tried leaving water in with them, but I soon discovered that they enjoyed turning the container over, resulting in soggy beds and wasted straw. It was an awful job and one I did not look forward to. I must have carted thousands of gallons of water over the years, and removed many gallons from the kitchen floor!

Another winter job, which Jim had to do, was the cutting up of hay-stacks into trusses ready for selling. A truss of new hay weighed sixty pounds and a truss of old hay fifty-six. He started at one end of a hay-stack by removing part of the thatch, and then with a very sharp hay knife the trusses would be cut out. They measured about three feet by two feet and one foot thick. There was an outsized skewer which was stuck into the middle of a truss so that the hay could be slid off the stack and car-ried down the ladder resting on Jim's hip. On the ground I had laid out the lengths of binder twine on to which Jim put the truss ready for tying up. Unfortunately there was a bit of loss because the hay immediately under the thatch was usually spoilt, as was any in contact with the ground. It was definitely better to stack it in a Dutch barn, which was no more than a roof supported on uprights; or in a barn. I loved the sight of haystacks, but one had to be realistic.

Clover was dry by the middle of January 1946 and Mr Fitch bought her for the price I paid, which was very kind of him considering she was in calf to an Ayrshire bull. At the end of March he phoned to say she had had a bull calf.

Jersey also had a bull calf, in February, and she calved so quickly and easily that none of us knew anything about it. When I let her out in the morning I thought she might give birth soon, but it was only when I went to call her in for her evening feed that I realised something must have hap-pened. She was down at the bottom of the field, almost out of sight in the corner where the land dipped a bit. She looked up when I called and then put her head down to something hidden from view. I went to look and there was Jersey's first calf. Jersey was easy to milk. Massaging her udder had paid off handsomely and I never had any trouble with her, except when the bats were about. I didn't discover her disliking for them until one evening in October. Jersey walked into the barn as two bats came fly-ing towards her at about knee level. She shied to one side to avoid them, which made them do some incredible aerobatics. Had she kept going they would have changed course to miss her without any fuss. As it was, her action caused one to fly between her front legs and the other to skim along her side. She was horrified. I tied her up and fetched her food, the milking stool and the pail. She wouldn't eat her food because the bats were prov-ing to be too much of a distraction. She wanted to escape and backed to the limits of her tether, tail lashing all the time. I pulled her back up to

My parents with Michael. 1947.

the manger, sat down on the stool and tried to milk her. She backed away again and aimed a kick at a bat that had just flown under her tummy. Her foot ended in the pail so I took her out to the brick shed and milked her there. Fortunately the bats were not constant visitors and sometimes several days went by before they put in another appearance. While they were about they were very active and had all the cats and dogs watching them with considerable interest.

For years we had stored the onions in the barn, hanging ropes of them high above the manger, only taking them into Meadow View when the frosts came. Rose had never touched them, but to our dismay Jersey did. She just managed to stretch up far enough to wrap her tongue round the lowest onion of one rope and with one good pull had most of them in the manger. She ate them with relish. I returned with the bucket and milking stool and found one cow with watering eyes munching hard and smelling strongly of onions. We decided she had eaten at least a dozen large onions, and her milk next day was appalling! Only hunger made the calves drink it. They kept stopping and coming off the teat, sniffing it and then sucking again. I thoroughly sympathised with them but they had to have it.

Jersey's bull calf had been sold at about one week old and I then bought the last two heifers I would rear. They were crossbred Ayrshires: one was half shorthorn and I think the other was half Jersey. I remember it was a very pale calf and I wondered how well it would do. That was the one which ate Mum's hankie when it slipped out of her sleeve as she was leaning over the partition in the barn to admire the latest arrivals. It was a very pretty lace-edged hankie and though I grabbed the calf and opened its mouth, I was too late.

Jersey's milk was wonderful, with thick, pale, richly flavoured cream. Her butter was quite different from Rose's, being almost white in comparison, and softer. I never had a butterfat count done but I wouldn't have been surprised if it had not been higher than Rose's. She was a very good milker and produced four and a half gallons a day for at least the first two months, perhaps due to the quarter of shorthorn blood in her veins. Unfortunately she was always a timid cow, gentle and easy to handle as long as one wasn't rough or quick. Unexpected things frightened her and she was not very inquisitive. Not like Rose, who always wanted to know what was happening, and had to examine everything. I don't remember Rose ever being afraid.

Sue and I did our last odd jobs for Frank early in April. Then Peter was home, and I stopped working at Tuffs Farm. I had been there for five years. In many ways I was sorry to leave. I knew I would miss the work and the friends I had made, but it was time to settle down to married life. I would be twenty-six in July and wanted to start a family.

We took up residence in the cottage at the end of April and bought our first lot of utility furniture: a double bed, a wardrobe and two easy chairs. That was all we could afford but luckily I had been given a single bed, a wardrobe and dressing table for my eighteenth birthday, and we took those to the cottage. Fortunately Mum had kept the gate-legged table and four chairs which had been in the playroom at Whippendell House, and she gave them to us.

The cottage was very small but suited our needs admirably. Upstairs there was one medium-size room with two minute ones leading off it. Our double bed just fitted in one and the single bed in the other. The kitchen was so small that two of us could barely fit in it. It had a sink and two draining boards, some shelves and a minute gas cooker. The larder was between the bathroom and kitchen. There was a small hall and a living room which was big enough to take our easy chairs, the table and four chairs, and, when we could finally afford them, a small sideboard and a desk. We settled in happily and remained there until April 1951.

Shortly before Peter came home I asked Mr Martin if I could, once more, use one of his Ayrshire bulls to serve Jersey. To my dismay he told me that the Ministry of Agriculture had just brought in a ruling preventing all tuberculin-tested bulls from serving cows from outside their own farms. This measure was taken as a means of eradicating tuberculosis. Though my cows were tuberculin-tested every year, and always passed the test, they were, nevertheless, regarded as a potential hazard to any other herd.

This was a terrible blow and meant artificial insemination, which was just beginning to gain in popularity. Fortunately there was a centre near at hand, in Aylesbury I think, and they could provide semen from a pedigree Jersey bull. I booked them for the next date when Jersey would be in season and said I would phone to confirm, the minute she was ready. The day arrived and a very pleasant young man turned up with a van full of the necessary equipment. He washed his hands carefully in the kitchen; put on a large overall and I took him to meet Jersey. She was tied up in the barn, waiting his ministrations. She glanced at him casually, probably thinking he was the vet, acquiesced in all he did to her and made no complaint. It was quick, efficient and Jersey was not in season again, so it had all been most effective. I was very pleased because, if we could have a heifer, it would be only one eighth shorthorn this time and ought to be even better then Jersey.

Mum had at last decided to cut back on rabbit production and she sold half the breeding does and one buck. The twelve does had been producing four families each a year, which was a total of forty-eight litters, probably averaging ten rabbits a litter. Spitfire and Hurricane produced twelve rabbits every time, but they were exceptional. The young rabbits had been particularly useful during the spring and summer months, because when they were about a month old they went outside into converted chicken arks and were able to run on the lawn and eat the grass. Every day the arks were moved onto a new patch. With fewer rabbits to help there would be more lawn mowing to do.

In the middle of May I began to feel unwell: my glands were swollen, I had a slight temperature and was decidedly off-colour. The doctor examined me, and pronounced that I had a mild infection, which he thought would run its course in a week or two. I felt tired and was very thankful that I was no longer working – at least I could be lazy all day, apart from the milking and calf feeding.

A week went by and I felt no better, so I complained to the doctor again. This time one of his partners visited me. He took one look at me and said he wouldn't be surprised if I was pregnant. Tests were done and the mild infection was correctly diagnosed. I was pregnant, and the baby was due on 9th February 1947.

By now Peter was on a business training course, which lasted until October, when he joined Cooper McDougall and Robertson in Berkhamsted. We were delighted that he had found a job near at hand: now we would not have to leave Chipperfield for a while. Fortunately in those days there were plenty of buses so Peter was able to reach Berkhamsted quite easily. He usually left at 7.45 in the morning and was home by 7.15 in the evening.

During the winter Peter and I began planning the small garden we would have at the front of the cottage. We fenced it off with chestnut fencing, to make a secure place in which to leave the pram, and Peter also decided to grow loganberries where the air-raid shelter had been dug for the evacuees. It entailed filling in the six-foot-deep trench, with hardcore for drainage, masses of earth and lots of manure. It took several weekends to complete but the resulting bed was excellent and the loganberries it grew were marvellous.

Jersey and I had timed our pregnancies very well because by the time I could no longer sit comfortably on the stool to milk her, she had dried up. The problem was going to arise when she calved, in about the middle of January 1947.

She had her calf one evening and I was not allowed to be present. I was told by everyone that to watch a cow giving birth could start me off, which was not a good idea because I still had three weeks to go. So I spent the time leaning out of a bedroom window, trying to see into the open barn, where Jersey was giving birth, until I became too cold! Tom was watching over her and Mrs Martin had said she would come down if her help was needed. But Jersey produced yet another big bull with no difficulty at all. When it was all over I was allowed to see the calf and make sure Jersey was all right. Tom moved them both into the big barn for the night, where they would be warm, and that was when I had a bright idea. I decided that until I was fit and able to do the milking the calf would be left with Jersey all night, which meant it would be getting a good supply of milk. During the day Jersey would be out until Tom arrived, which was about five o'clock. Then she would be milked, but not completely, and returned to the calf. It worked very well, apart from them mooing at one another in the afternoon, when the calf began to feel peckish. I was sure my baby would be born on February the 9th and equally sure that I would be doing the milking a fortnight later. My best-laid plans went wrong.

I should have attended Jersey's confinement to speed things up, because Michael was ten days late. Unfortunately I had a long and difficult labour and was told to take things very easily for at least two months. Consequently, the calf spent the nights with Jersey until well into April. It grew at a great pace so I decided that the sensible thing to do was to fatten him and sell him at about ten months old. Now that I had a baby to look after I didn't want the extra work of heifer calves again.

The calf was christened Baby Bull and he turned out to be a cheerful, playful animal – a true extrovert. When the weather was warm enough for him to go out he dashed around playing with Rufus and Paddy, and even tried to make Sue play too. Fortunately I had had the sense to get him used to a halter and was able to lead him from one bit of grazing to another without him galloping all over the place. He was practically all black, which brought back memories of Miss Hawes' angry black cow. What Cosmo would have thought of him I do not know! We occasionally did mock bull fights with him, which were great fun. He never attacked us but he would tear around and rush up to us, snorting and lowing his front end, rather like a dog. He did look funny. Then it was our turn and we would pretend to attack him and he would go dashing off, tail held high. We had lots of fun with Baby Bull and were very sorry to see him go. He was a very big ten-month-old bull and I seem to remember he fetched twenty pounds as baby beef.

The incredible summer of 1947 was partly responsible for his excellent growth I'm sure, as well as the quantities of good Jersey milk he had drunk. Michael also benefited from the glorious weather and for many weeks he was out in his pram until the ten o'clock feed at night.

Back in April I had arranged for Jersey to be inseminated again, but unfortunately it had to be the same Jersey bull. I wanted a change as I was still after the elusive heifer! The same young man turned up but when he approached Jersey he had a very different reception. She took one look at him and arched her back. He spoke to her soothingly, to no avail. We scratched her back in the hopes that she would dip it. She refused.

"Take her for a walk and I'll try again as soon as you bring her back," he suggested. Jersey was walked round the drive and back towards the barn. The minute she saw him she stopped, before we had even reached the barn, and arched her back. I walked her round again and he hid. I brought her back to the barn, tied her up and put some food in the manger, while he tried taking her by surprise. That failed. Jersey's tail was clamped down hard, like an iron bar, while her back remained obstinately arched. We were ages with her but in the end we had to admit defeat. The young man said he had never seen anything like it. So Jersey would become another barren cow and there was nothing I could do. There were other, untested bulls in the neighbourhood, but Jersey was tuberculin free and I didn't want to take any risks. I was sad: she would milk until about November, or December with luck, and then it would be the knacker's yard for her. It seemed such an awful waste – she had only had two calves and was a very good milker.

Michael with Rufus, Paddy and Jill.

We did not bother to grow any hay in 1947 so Sue, Baby Bull and Jersey had plenty of grazing. I felt I was being lazy after the previous hectic five years but looking after a baby seemed to keep me well occupied.

During August, Peter's brother Raymond stayed with us for about a week. One day he announced, in all seriousness, that he would ride Sue down to Kings Langley, where there was a very good cake shop. He had a yearning for currant buns. We all recommended that he should go by bus, or use one of our bicycles, because Sue had not done any work or been ridden for many months. Ray was determined. He said the exercise would do them both a lot of good.

To my surprise Sue behaved herself while she was given a quick grooming and made no fuss when the saddle was put on. I had expected her to be a bit restless. She didn't do anything alarming when Ray mounted, and they set off quite happily for Kings Langley. Ray went the back way, down the lane and through all the fields, eventually joining the road near Barnes Farm, where Mr Martin lived. She had never been ridden to Kings Langley so when she reached the place where I always turned and headed for home, she swung round and started to trot back. Ray had a terrible struggle to make her continue to Kings Langley. He finally won and trotted on his way. Then, much to his annoyance, Sue began shying at all the traffic. When he eventually reached the shop, having had to walk her for the last several hundred yards along the main road, he had to stand outside to make his purchase. Sue was jumpy and nervous, ears twitching all the time, and she wouldn't stand still. He bought half a dozen big currant buns and set off on his return journey. She had quietened a bit by now, but not enough to make for a pleasant ride and Ray decided to stuff the bag of buns down his shirt to leave both hands free.

With her nose heading towards home Sue stepped out. Cobs are not the most comfortable of horses to ride – their stride is short and can be a bit jerky. I always found I had to hang on tight when Sue cantered and Ray had to do just that. She pounded her way home and arrived back very out of breath. Ray looked dishevelled and the currant buns looked even worse. They had been flattened and needed a bit of pulling into shape before we could toast them. He had been gone for hours.

"What on earth kept you?" Peter asked him, rather tactlessly.

"This wretched horse," he replied. "She was awful. She nearly threw me on one occasion."

"I did warn you she hadn't been worked or ridden for ages," I said.

"I know," replied Ray, "but I didn't expect her to be that bad!"

seen so many loganberries. The following year they were so full of maggots we couldn't eat any. Not to be beaten, I decided to make loganberry
jelly. We removed as many maggots as possible, simmered the loganberries in very little water to draw out all the juice, and strained the pulp
through muslin to remove the remaining maggots; and there were still an
awful lot. It was as much as Mum could do to try our jelly after our graphic
descriptions. Pa didn't help by saying the added protein would be nourish-
ing. However, the resulting jelly was quite fantastic.

I had just adjusted to life with only hens, cats and dogs, when Peter
heard about "Goat Dairies", who were looking for people to supply them
with milk. We contacted them, found out how much they paid per pint, and
decided to buy two goats. There was a growing market for goat's milk and
we thought it might bring in a little much-needed money.

I knew nothing about goats, but was sure they would be no more difficult than cows. The first surprise was the size of their teats. I thought
they would be a little bigger than sheep's teats and imagined I would only
be using my first finger and thumb for milking, but their teats were fatter
than a cow's and the milk poured out very easily. Milking was done in a
few minutes.

The first goat we bought, called Bimba, was supposed to be in kid.
Two weeks went by and nothing happened. The woman from whom we
had bought her was very unpleasant and quite rude to Peter. She refused to
take Bimba back, or to offer any reduction in price. We were furious and
had to find a billy goat as quickly as we could. Luckily there was another
couple in Chipperfield who also kept goats and they put us in touch with
the owners of a billy in Bushey. Getting Bimba there was going to be a
problem. Finally, the owner of a taxi in Kings Langley offered his serv-
ices. We were most grateful and he was very brave to risk transporting a
goat in his car! Dozens of big sacks were spread all over the floor and seat
and, to Peter's relief, Bimba did not disgrace herself by eating the uphol-
stery during the journey. He was surprised at how well she behaved. The
mating was successful, but we had to wait four months for the kid to be
born and milk production was very low. Our idea was not proving to be
very successful, so we bought another goat. This one had horns and a tendency for mountaineering, but at least she was a good milker. She could
get out of almost anywhere, so Peter had to alter the old calf pen in the
big barn to make it goat proof. It was like a fortress, and when the goat
wasn't outside grazing she was in the pen. One big advantage with goats is
that they can be tethered and left to graze everything in reach. We found

147

it most useful and had them grazing the lawns, which did help in cutting down the number of times they had to be mown. Goats are also browsers and they enjoy almost everything in a garden, so a watchful eye had to be kept on them to make sure their tethers were so placed that they couldn't reach any of Mum's nice shrubs.

Bimba produced two billy kids. Yet again the females eluded us. We kept the kids for a short time and then Tom killed them and we ate them. Milk production was good and we were nicely into the swing of things, when Goat Dairies went out of business and we had to sell up.

In April 1951 Peter, Michael and I moved to Amersham, taking Jill and six hens with us. Two months later Elizabeth was born and in October my parents moved to Hampstead. Our links with the countryside were severed.

I had enjoyed nearly twenty years of country life and the move into a small town, while being welcome in some respects, represented a loss of freedom. I missed the peace and quiet, the farmyard sounds and smells (even the powerful ones!), the animals and, above all, the country people. On the plus side was the nearness of the shops, the doctor and the schools, and also a good train service to London. Sadly, there would be no more bats in my bedroom.

Postscript

It is now sixty-two years since I stopped working at Tuffs Farm. It is still going strong, I am glad to say. Jim took over the farm from his father in 1965 and expanded it, by buying some fields near Tenements Farm. He is eighty-six and his son Roger now runs it. Georgie was killed in action in Germany in February 1945 aged eighteen, and is buried in the Reichswald Forest War Cemetery. Jim and his wife Daphne have, over the years, visited and been visited by the family in Belgium with whom Georgie was billeted for a while. It has helped to ease the pain. Georgie would be eighty-two now.

All the land is down to grass for haymaking. No more horses, and all the equipment is huge and modern. Does the job in half the time now! There was something peaceful about working with horses, when they behaved themselves! Also, it was quiet.

Sadly, shortly after Jim had helped with this postscript he had a third heart attack and died. I had so hoped he would have lived long enough to see the book.

Anthea Hanscomb
October 2008